T0143430

CYBERSECURITY PUBLIC POLICY

CYBERSECURITY PUBLIC POLICY

SWOT Analysis Conducted on 43 Countries

Bradley Fowler
Kennedy Maranga

CRC Press
Taylor & Francis Group
Boca Raton New York London

CRC Press is an imprint of the
Taylor & Francis Group, an **informa** business

First edition published 2022
by CRC Press
6000 Broken Sound Parkway NW, Suite 300, Boca Raton, FL 33487-2742

and by CRC Press
4 Park Square, Milton Park, Abingdon, Oxon, OX14 4RN

CRC Press is an imprint of Taylor & Francis Group, LLC

ISBN: 978-1-032-19433-2 (hbk)
ISBN: 978-1-032-19434-9 (pbk)
ISBN: 978-1-003-25914-5 (ebk)

DOI: 10.1201/9781003259145

Typeset in Caslon
by SPi Technologies India Pvt Ltd (Straive)

Contents

Acknowledgements

In 2008, I began studying Computer Information Systems at Penn Foster College online, in an Associate of Science degree program; I never fathomed it would take fourteen years to gain as much clarity on computers, cybersecurity, and cybersecurity policy as I have. Over these last fourteen years, many public and private sectors have experienced cyber-attacks. Despite the efforts to hire qualified information technology (IT) and cybersecurity practitioners to help deter such attacks, threats remain uncontained. Thus, I have acquired a desire to help educate people about cybersecurity and the value of creating and implementing effective cybersecurity policy that deters unauthorized attacks and stops cybercrime. This work is a creative means of sharing my education, knowledge, skills, and ability to develop, implement, and manage cybersecurity strategies and cybersecurity policy. My work here aligns with the education I've acquired in the Master of Science in Managing Information Systems, specializing in Information Security Management, attained from Bellevue University, where I earned a 3.940 GPA in August 2021, as well as a Master of Public Policy in Cybersecurity Policy conferred by the American Public University System, which I earned with a 3.969 GPA in September 2020. Prior to completing these degree programs, I earned a Master of Science in Cybersecurity at Bellevue University in June 2018 with a 3.956 GPA, as well as a Master of Arts in Teaching and Learning with Technology from Ashford University in October 2016, where I earned a 4.00 GPA. In January 2021, I enrolled in a Master of Science in Cloud Computing Architecture at the University of Maryland Global Campus, which will be conferred by the release of this textbook. And by the time this book is released for retail purchase, I will be All But Dissertation in a Doctor of Education Administration, which I'm acquiring from California Coast University.

Attaining education in these subjects has been eye-opening; as much as I am sure learning about cybersecurity and cybersecurity public policy will be for millions around the globe, who rely on the Internet and computer devices to communicate, develop, and create documents, store and retrieve data; and transmit and read sensitive information. However, without government protection of our usage of technology and the Internet, we remain vulnerable to cyber-attacks deployed by militias, religious groups, governments, individuals, state actors, nation states, and organized criminals. Thus, it is critical that we each take a sincere approach to understand the role we play as global citizens in protecting our information assets from cybercriminals.

Thus, I must acknowledge the United States White House for updating and sharing the National Cyber Strategy in January 2018. This National Cyber Strategy provides the American people a gateway of clarity regarding the methods being deployed by the United States Department of Homeland Security (DHS), National Security Agency (NSA), U.S. Military, and local law enforcement, to protect citizens' right to rely on technology in their daily lives, to achieve their goals and meet their organizational missions. I also would like to acknowledge the Information Systems Audit and Control Association (ISACA), for continuing to disseminate its informative digital newsletter that shares valued information about cybersecurity around the globe, and what is happening to help fight and deter cyber-attacks. Furthermore, I acknowledge the National Cybersecurity Student Association, BitSight Technologies for their Gartner Cybersecurity Report, Cyberspace Solarium Commission, the National Conference of State Legislatures Cybersecurity Legislature 2019, the National Institute of Standards and Technology (NIST), Info-Security Magazine, the SANS Institute, Global Cybersecurity Index, Global Cybersecurity Agenda, Global Security Review, Global Cyber Alliance, Global Cybersecurity Capacity Centre, and the Information Systems Security Association. Additionally, I would like to acknowledge all Alumni from Bellevue University, Ashford University, American Public University System, and the University of Maryland Global Campus who have completed cybersecurity, managing information systems, cybersecurity public policy, and cloud computing architecture program studies at these dynamic learning institutions.

Bradley Fowler, MA, MSc, MPP, MMIS
October 2021

List of Abbreviations

AI	Artificial Intelligence
CEO	Chief Executive Officer
CERT	Computer Emergency Response Team
CI	Computer Information
CIA	Confidentiality, Integrity, and Availability
CIAA	Confidentiality, Integrity, Availability, and Accountability
CIO	Chief Information Officer
COO	Chief Operating Officer
CTO	Chief Technology Officer
CYBEX	Cybersecurity Information Exchange Techniques
DDOSA	Distributed Denial of Service Attack
DHS	Department of Homeland Security
EU	European Union
GDPR	General Data Protection Regulation
HIPAA	Health Insurance Portability and Accountability Act
IaaS	Infrastructure as a Service
ICT	Information Communication Technology
IOT	Internet of Things
ISACA	Information Systems Audit and Control Association
ISP	Internet Service Provider
IT	Information Technology
SaaS	Software as a Service

SDK	Software Development Kit
SSL	Security Socket Layer
SWOT	Strength Weakness Opportunities Threats
NATO	North Atlantic Treaty Organization
NCSS	National Cyber Security Strategy
NIPR	Net-Non-Classified IP Router Network
NIST	National Institute of Standards and Technology
NSA	National Security Agency
PaaS	Platform as a Service
UK	United Kingdom
UN	United Nations

Understanding the words that embody cybersecurity gives you power to deter and defeat cybercriminals.

– LaShawn Fowler

Author Biographies

Bradley Fowler earned a Master of Public Policy in Cybersecurity Policy from American Public University System in 2020, a Master of Science in Cybersecurity in 2018, and a Master of Science in Managing Information Systems in Information Security Management in 2021, both from Bellevue University. Bradley also earned a Master of Arts in Teaching and Learning with Technology in 2016 and a Bachelor of Arts in eMarketing in 2015, both from Ashford University, which is now part of the University of Arizona Global Campus. Bradley is graduating from the University of Maryland Global Campus with a Master of Science in Cloud Computing Architecture and will be ABD-i.e., All But Dissertation in a Doctor of Education Administration from California Coast University in 2022.

Bradley is a member of the Golden Key International Honour Society, National Cybersecurity Alliance, and the National Cybersecurity Student Association. He has been a contributing writer for the National Security Policy Analysis Organization since January 2020 and owns Construction eMarketing.

Bradley's hobbies include: weight training, roller skating, traveling, cooking, and writing non-fiction and fiction works, as well as conducting scholarly research on cybersecurity public policy worldwide and domestic educational policy.

Dr. Kennedy Maranga is a Doctoral Dissertation Chair and Associate Professor in the School of Leadership, Education, and Communication at St. Thomas University. Dr. Maranga lives in St. Louis MO and holds a Bachelor of Laws degree, Master of Science in Higher Education Administration from Walden University, Masters of Laws from Washington University St. Louis, and Ph.D in Public Policy and Administration from Walden University. Dr. Maranga enjoys teaching and mentoring learners. Professional experience over the last 25 years includes working as a professor, an attorney, consultant, and president of a non-profit organization. Dr. Maranga has a strong background and interest in both qualitative and quantitative methods and designs. He has authored and co-authored several peer-reviewed articles and three books. In his free time he enjoys reading, writing, and from time to time, traveling across the globe.

INTRODUCTION

Cybersecurity plays a central role in supporting the security of our society. However, the term cybersecurity is not defined straightforwardly. Over the years, cybersecurity has become increasingly cross-border making it challenging to grasp its full purpose and dimensions at a glance.

In fact, cybersecurity is constantly evolving just as much as threats and vulnerabilities. There is no single best approach for government entities to protect themselves against all forms of cybercrime. This book examines, compares, and describes 43 countries cybersecurity public policy utilizing a SWOT Analysis. This book sheds light about cybersecurity, cybercrime, cybersecurity public policy, and mitigation strategies that are available for countries to effectively manage and protect their technology tools, hardware, software, computers, virtual environments, as well as to help you understand how these 43 countries have defined cybersecurity policies to protect their citizens from cybersecurity compromises.

The development of the internet is characterized with unlimited vulnerabilities. A wide set of public policy initiatives are defined to ensure integrity and confidentiality are maintained. Therefore, there should be no doubt that increasing and emerging threats are parallel with new technologies and certainly require innovative and carefully designed public policy and vulnerability and threat mitigation measures. Countries must therefore invest and work collaboratively with others to strengthen security. Cyberattacks are usually engulfed in financial gain among other motives. Attacks are always feasible as no system can claim to be secure. Thus, the goal of any cybersecurity

DOI: 10.1201/9781003259145-1

public policy comes down to identifying the risks, the potential impact of an attack, and how to protect against attacks.

This book describes cybersecurity public policy approaches from 43 different countries and examines the evolution and practice of cybersecurity and cybercrime from the advent of the digital era to the present day. This book also shares public policy recommendations on cybersecurity for the future needs of our global society.

1

INTRODUCTION TO CYBERSECURITY

Learning Objectives

- Comprehend the meaning of cybersecurity.
- Understand why cybersecurity is invaluable to the safety of Internet users.
- Discover the impact of cybersecurity internationally.
- Understand why cybersecurity must align with public and private sector.

Cybersecurity has been defined differently across America and around the world. In the United States, many confuse cybersecurity with information technology, network security, or information security. The United States Cybersecurity & Infrastructure Security Agency defines cybersecurity as the "artistic approach to protect networks, devices, and data from unauthorized access or criminal usage and the practice of deploying confidentiality, integrity, and availability of information assets".[1] The European Union definition of cybersecurity encompasses all activities required to protect cyberspace, cyberspace users, and all persons impacted from cyber threats.[2] In India, the definition of cybersecurity is the protection of computers, networks, programs, and data from unauthorized access or attacks that are aimed at exploitation.[3] Thus, the meaning of cybersecurity differs greatly around the world, but requires the same mitigation strategies and risk management approach, no matter what geographical location the subject matter is discussed. Everyone who relies on technology, mobile devices, software, hardware, and virtual cloud environments has heard of cybersecurity. So, why do so many people around the world have a nonchalant attitude about the value and importance of cybersecurity. After all, no industry is without the reliance upon technology tools, virtual cloud environments, software, hardware, artificial

DOI: 10.1201/9781003259145-2

intelligence, Internet of Things, 3D printing, quantum computing, and cybersecurity.

In fact, today cybersecurity and technology tools, virtual cloud environments, software, hardware, artificial intelligence, Internet of Things, 3D printing, and quantum computing, impacts eleven sectors (e.g., energy, materials, industrials, consumer discretionary, consumer staples, health care, financials, information technology, communications services, utilities, and real estate). These sectors can be divided into industry groups, industries, and subindustries. The sector with the highest integration of technology is health. Second is financial. Technology is third and industries are fourth. Of all these sectors, cybersecurity strategies must align with each sector and be a pivotal component in protecting the information assets developed, stored, shared, and electronically transmitted across the Internet. Unless each sector has its own cybersecurity team of experts working closely within their daily workplace; each sector takes the chance of being victimized by cyberattacks, cyber-terrorist, cyber-criminals, cyber-bullies, cyber-espionage, and cyber-stalkers. Therefore, cybersecurity is essential.

One way to begin understanding cybersecurity is learning the difference between information security and information assets. Having knowledge on each of these subjects provides clarity on cybersecurity and the role cybersecurity plays in protecting information and information assets. In fact, when evaluating the value of information within any sector, service providers typically attain, share, and store consumer information, regardless if that information is public or private. Consumers rely on service providers to render special care for whatever reason the consumer seeks to have their needs or wants met. In many instances, the information is the value of the service being rendered. For instance, when a consumer seeks understanding of a subject matter such as the law, they turn to an attorney, legal advisor, or paralegal. The services provided are offered in the information these experts possess. The same can be applied to health care. The doctor or nurse provides the patient with information to improve health issues. The information also enables the patient to gain understanding on what is required to achieve the end results, they seek to manage their medical or health issue. The exchange of information provided by these trusted sources is what makes the information an asset of the service provider.

When a product developer designs a new product, information is developed and printed on paper and packaged for the consumer, with hopes of providing the consumer details about the design and creation of the product. This is intellectual property. The information or design model is the asset, the product developer wants to secure and keep confidential from consumers, so the product developer maintains control over the information asset and the key ingredients to produce the product. Cybersecurity practitioner's role is to help the service and product manufacturers maintain control and security over the information assets, they own, store on information systems, and share with others, either in written format, digitally, or electronically. The information asset is what is being protected. Cybersecurity practitioners deploy a strategy that enables service and product developers and providers, to secure their information secrets and keep them safe from those who seek to steal or duplicate the information assets, the service or product provider places value on.

When deploying cybersecurity for public or private sector, the approach is always the same. No matter the value of information, the strategies, assessments, plans, and mitigation strategies do not change. After all, cybersecurity practitioners protect the information created, stored, and shared online across the Internet. Cybersecurity co-exists with information security, information technology, virtual cloud environments, software, hardware, artificial intelligence, Internet of Things, 3D printing, and quantum computing. Today, many sectors rely on information technology to conduct workplace activities. These activities include transmitting trade secrets, sending money via electronic transmission with the assistance of technology payment terminals. For example, banks enable account holders to establish banking accounts and save their personal authentication log-in information in an encrypted format, with assurance their banking data will be secure once they log offline and during all online transactions. Cybersecurity practitioners deploy effective methods that provide the security to protect technology and the information assets, exchanged and transmitted via the Internet.

If any sector or industry relies on technology, there is a need for cybersecurity. The two support each other. After all, technology is a primary component of cybersecurity. The keyword is cyber. Cambridge Dictionary defines cyber as "involving, using, or relating to computers, especially the Internet".[4] Thus, without effective mitigation methods to secure the information assets of the enterprise, the enterprise's daily workplace operations and information systems can experience catastrophic impact. This can be costly, especially if damage impacts the reputation of the enterprise, its services, or product (s). It can also be damaging to the technology tools (e.g., virtual cloud environments, software, hardware, artificial intelligence, Internet of Things, 3D printing, and quantum computing) relied upon and cost tremendously to restore the technology damaged.

Recent events in cyberattacks have cost some sectors more than $500 million. In fact, The Home Office Science Advisory Council in the United Kingdom reported in its Research Report 96 titled *Understanding the Costs of Cybercrime: A report of key findings from the Costs of Cyber Crime Working Group*, that a "top-end estimate of £27 billion for economic cost to the UK".[5] In India, cybercrime cost on average $20 million. In Asia, it was reported that "cyberattacks on Asian Ports could cost as much as $100 billion".[6] Thus, it is time to take a closer look at understanding cybersecurity and its role in helping thwart unwanted cyberattacks.

In fact, cyberattacks have grown exponentially and now bridge several landscapes of international crime. Cyber terrorism is the use of technology and the Internet to deploy threats and conduct attacks that often result in the loss of large monetary units, property, or human life. Cyber terrorism is a form of cyberattack that can be orchestrated from any geographical location worldwide and deployed with the use of technology, including software, hardware, virtual cloud environments, artificial intelligence, Internet of Things, 3D printing, quantum computing, and satellite. When former President George W. Bush sought to locate Saddam Hussein, not only were drowns deployed, but satellites were utilized to help canvas the geographical location in search of this terrorist. Cyber terrorists can launch attacks from beyond international borders without legal retaliation from many legal territories. Due to this growing phenomenon, there is a need to increase the penalties for cyber terrorism and develop and implement effective cybersecurity policy that helps deter and hopefully, decrease the number of successful cyber-terrorist attacks. However, due to many countries' inability to effectively communicate with other countries, attain, train, and educate citizens within their countries, there remains a huge gap in the development and implementation of effective cybersecurity law and public policy.

Thus, many countries are implementing strategies to overcome the seemingly endless attacks deployed against their citizens and public/private sectors. This has helped enable a growth of communication between governments, Parliaments, Ministries, and political leaders, in search of defining an effective approach to govern and control cybercrime, cyberterrorism, cyberbullying, cyberstalking, cyberattacks, and cyber espionage. One way that has proven successful in bridging the gap of communication, is establishing a treaty on cybersecurity. This has been initiated by The International Law Commission and the International Telecommunication Union. However, when considering the enactment of a Treaty encompassing cybersecurity, it is important to also consider the lack of authority international law may have. Thus, to achieve a Treaty on cybersecurity, requires an international agreement defined by the authorities who enact international laws. Even though international efforts to implement effective cybersecurity law and policy continue being evaluated, developed, implemented, and managed. A successful approach to enacting cybersecurity policy has fallen into the hands of each country; rendering control over the development, implementation, and management of cybersecurity policy as the force to govern all cybersecurity incidence. As a result, tremendous research has been deployed to provide the public with clarity on cybersecurity and cybersecurity policy. In rendering this quality of enlightenment, the public can gain essential knowledge of their role and responsibilities in helping deter and thwart cyberattacks.

In the United States, the U.S. Department of Homeland Security, the National Security Agency, as well as the White House, have assessed, developed, and implemented national security cybersecurity policy that educates Americans on the strategies being deployed to effectively protect the liberty of Americans who rely on technology and the Internet for economic stability and personal growth. In fact, former President Donald J. Trump signed the revised version of the National Security Cyber Strategy in January 2018, confirming an alliance between the U.S. Department of Homeland Security, National Security Agency, and the White House, as well as both public and private sector. This National Cyber Strategy continues being the bedrock of America's effective approach to combating unauthorized access of public information systems securing federal information data. Such policy can be an effective model for private sector to mirror and international governments, Parliaments, Ministries, and political leaders to assess, revise, and implement in alignment with the current national security cybersecurity policy, they have developed and are relying on. However, for national security cybersecurity policy to be effective, it requires teamwork. This teamwork encompasses country political leaders, ambassadors, governments, educators, private and public sector managers, CEO, CTO, CIO, COO, and VP, as well as citizens to work in concert, to achieve the end goal…defending the privacy rights of all who rely on the Internet as their primary gateway to connect with the world and share their business and personal information worldwide.

To achieve this goal requires understanding why cybersecurity is essential. Research compiled by the United States Council of Economic Advisors convey that

> scarce data and insufficient information sharing impede cybersecurity efforts and slow down the development of the cyber insurance market. Cybersecurity is a common good; lax cybersecurity imposes negative externalities on other economic entities and on private citizens. Failure to account for these negative externalities results in under-investment in cybersecurity by the private sector relative to the socially optimal level of investment.[7]

Thus, to effectively protect the information assets of both public and private sector, the installation of clearly conveyed cybersecurity policy is required.

Today, 43 countries have already taken steps to develop and implement clearly written cybersecurity public policy, in the universal English speaking and writing language. However, due to the differences in the type of cyberattacks, cyber terrorism, cyberbullying, cybercrime, and cyber espionage deployed against each country, one national security cybersecurity policy does not meet the needs of all 43 countries. Even worse, due to the low level of experienced and knowledgeable cybersecurity experts within these 43 countries, the tasks of effectively implementing cybersecurity and staying current with trends encompassing cybercrime, cyber terrorism, cyber espionage, cyberattacks, and cyberbullying, countries are desperately seeking help. This book is a resource of help that will enable these 43 countries to gain clarity on the importance of cybersecurity policy and how to define a clearly written cybersecurity policy that will be instrumental in educating both public and private sector.

According to the 2019 Official Annual Cybercrime Report developed by Steve Morgan, Editor and Chief of Cybersecurity Ventures, "cybercriminal activity is one of the biggest challenges that humanity will face in the next two decades".[8] There is no doubt that cybercriminals are taking the lead in controlling the dark market and dark web technology to launch their nefarious acts against public and private sector. To a degree that eventually will cost more than $30 trillion annually to combat. Thus, the race to define effective cybersecurity policy is on, and this race cannot be set aside. In fact, looking back to July 2015 when the United States Congress passed the Cyber Intelligence Sharing and Protection Act, it was perceived that this bill would facilitate the sharing of information security, especially information being transmitted across the Internet, between the federal government and private sector. Congress hoped this legislation would improve "information flow about information security threats and reduce risk to public infrastructure".[9]

This bill aligns with the Cybersecurity Information Sharing Act that requires the Director of National Intelligence, the Secretary of National Security, the Secretary of Defense, and the U.S. Attorney General, to define and promulgate procedures for classified and declassified cyber threat and vulnerability indicators in possession of the federal government, to be disseminated with private sector entities; non-government agencies, state, tribal, and local governments.[10] In the same year, former President Barack Obama signed the Cyber Sanctions Program into effect, to deploy an economic sanction, specifically on the seizure of U.S. based funds, against overseas attackers and organizations that willfully gain from cybercrime and cyber espionage.

This encouraged the establishment of the European Council of Cybercrime, who drafted the European Council Cybercrime Convention in 2001. This Convention gives an international task force the authority to oversee a plethora of Internet security methodologies and to standardize technology regulatory across international boundaries.

This also enables an improvement in international communication and data sharing between public and private sector, regarding cybercrime incidence. However, the European Council of Cybercrime does not embody the full authority to enact compliance with their implementation of cybercrime regulatory.

The same can be conveyed about the Digital Millennium Copyright Act, which is a U.S. based international effort to lower the impact of copyright, trademark, and privacy infringement, particularly encompassing the reduction of technological copyright protection methods. This policy installation invoked the European Council to adopt a similar approach, which they titled *The Database Right*. Furthermore, Australia has enacted the Commonwealth Legislation Part 10.7 titled *Computer Offences of the Criminal Code Act 1995*. Under the Act, laws provide protection for data system intrusion (e.g., hacking), unauthorized destruction or modification of data, as well as the development and distribution of intentional malicious software. Worldwide additional legislations are consistently being enacted, but until there are laws that govern the act of cybercrime, cyberattacks, cyber terrorism, and cyber espionage, cybersecurity public policy plays a pivotal role in governing many countries information technology, information systems, virtual cloud environments, software, hardware, artificial intelligence, Internet of Things, 3D printing, and quantum computing.

Unlike laws, policy must be enforced and shared with everyone that is expected to adhere to such. And since current cybersecurity policies being developed by each country differs, each country must take the initiative to update their cybersecurity policies annually and share this information with its citizens and internationally with governments, Parliaments, Ministries, and public and private sector. Doing so, enhances awareness of data sharing that enables a line of communication to be established, one that opens the door for feedback to be exchanged, and to invoke effective modifications to be implemented as necessary, to improve the current edition of each country's cybersecurity public policy. While cybersecurity policy can be instrumental in helping decrease attacks internationally, there must remain an essence of ethics in the development of these cybersecurity policies. After all, to achieve a global alliance of respect towards one country's cybersecurity public policy, all countries need to agree on a universal language of content. For example, some countries have published their cybersecurity public policy in their foreign language, such as China, Russia, and Morocco. Of course, the right to publish one's work as they see fit must be honored, but how can one country align its cybersecurity policy with another if there is a language barrier. Therefore, this research only provides a SWOT analysis on 43 countries' cybersecurity public policy. The willful lack of agreement to work in concert impacts the ability to understand the approach all countries are relying on to define, implement, and manage a clearly conveyed cybersecurity public policy.

Furthermore, it is just as important to address the primary needs of each country's cybersecurity infrastructure. Aligning the cybersecurity public policy with the needs of the country (e.g., type of crime deterrence necessary) helps define an effective security model that can be easily adopted and modified by other countries as they see fit, for their own cybersecurity public policy design. This SWOT analysis encompasses in-depth research of 43 countries' cybersecurity public policy and uncovers the strengths, weaknesses, opportunities, and threats enveloped within these public policies. Recommendations have been provided to help enhance these weaknesses and stamp out the known threats. It is essential that all cybersecurity public policy must be clearly conveyed and present the facts that enable each country to effectively implement risk management control that other countries can mirror.

Co-author Professor Kennedy Maranga, who earned his Doctor of Philosophy in Public Policy and a law degree, provided the introduction and shared case studies throughout this resource. Furthermore, I have utilized my education (e.g., Master of Science in Cybersecurity, Master of Science in Managing Information Systems, Master of Public Policy in Cybersecurity Policy, and Master of Arts in Teaching and Learning with Technology), 7 years experience, and research to educate public and private sector about cybersecurity public policy development, implementation, and usage. Utilizing a SWOT analysis enables the ability to convey clarity of the strengths, weaknesses, threats, and opportunities encompassed within these 43 countries' national security cybersecurity public policy. This research also shares need-to-know details regarding what cybersecurity is, as well as why cybersecurity policy should be a focus of private and public sector who utilize information technology, information systems, virtual cloud environments, software, hardware, artificial intelligence, Internet of Things, 3D printing, and quantum computing.

Summary

While the National Cyber Strategy of the United States signed in 2018 by former President Donald J. Trump has become the primary tool in helping define strategic methods to govern the current climate of cybersecurity within the United States. There remains a need to develop, implement, and manage effective risk management strategies, cybercrime laws, regulatory, and policy that will effectively manage workforce personnel hired to oversee public and private sector entities that rely on information systems, cloud environments, artificial intelligence, 3D printing, quantum computing, information technology, software, hardware, computers, telecommunication, and geospatial to conduct daily business operations that enable a free flow of data development, sharing, and storage, free of unauthorized tampering and modification. Without laws, regulatory, and policy to govern the development, implementation, sharing, and storage of personal and public data sources, information remains accessible and easy to utilize for nefarious purposes, without the proper authorization and with limited repercussion.

Thus, working diligently to enact new laws, regulatory, and policy in alignment with the needs of Congress and global governments, Parliaments, and Ministries, is essential to maintaining effective and efficient methodologies that help decrease the growing impact cybercrimes continue having on societies worldwide. This research is a gateway to understand what methods and cybersecurity public policy are being discussed and implemented to enable governments, Parliaments, Ministries, and authorized organizations and agencies to share cyber incident reports on cybercrimes being committed globally. Without these infrastructures there remains a continued threat that keeps our world entangled in darkness, impeding upon our privacy and usage of the Internet, information systems, broadband, WIFI, virtual cloud environments, 3D printing, artificial intelligence, Internet of Things, quantum computing, software, hardware, computers, telecommunication, and geospatial. Having clarity on the issues is vital to developing and implementing effective laws, regulatory, and policy that decreases these threats and help manage the need for increased budget spending to thwart unauthorized intrusion aiming to cripple global economies.

Discussion Questions

1. What does the United States Cybersecurity & Infrastructure Security Agency define cybersecurity as?
2. How many countries have taken steps to develop and implement cybersecurity public policy?
3. Can one cybersecurity policy meet the needs of all countries?
4. Who is taking the lead to control the dark web and technology?

Case Study

In January 2021, Country A, which was an advanced digital society suffered a series of cyberattacks targeted on governmental institutions. The cyberattacks lasted several weeks causing disruptions with national online public services. These attacks were not sophisticated and did not create lasting damage to Country A's digital infrastructure. However, they showed how cyberattacks take advantage of governments and could severely harm a country. These attacks helped shape Country A's cybersecurity public policy defense.

Based on what you have read in this chapter, what will be the most appropriate public policy defense and why?

Notes

1 What Is Cybersecurity? (2019). Cybersecurity & Infrastructure Security Agency. Retrieved from: https://uscert.cisa.gov/ncas/tips/ST04-001
2 ENISA Overview of Cybersecurity and Related Terminology. (2017). European Union Agency for Network and Information Security. Retrieved from: https://www.enisa.europa.eu/publications/enisa-position-papers-and-opinions/enisa-overview-of-cybersecurity-and-related-terminology
3 Definition of Cybersecurity. (2021). The Economic Times. Retrieved [3/22/2021] from: https://economictimes.indiatimes.com/definition/cyber-security
4 Definition of Cyber. (2021). Cambridge Dictionary. Retrieved from: https://dictionary.cambridge.org/us/dictionary/english/cyber

5 Goud, H. (2021). Cybersecurity Insiders. Cyber Attacks on Asian Ports Cost $110 Billion. Retrieved from: https://www.cybersecurity-insiders.com/cyber-attacks-on-asian-ports-cost-110-billion/#:~

6 Home Office Science Advisory Council. (2016). Understanding the Costs of Cybercrime. Retrieved from: https://assets.publishing.service.gov.uk/government/uploads/system/uploads/attachment_data/file/674046/understanding-costs-of-cyber-crime-horr96.pdf

7 Home Office Science Advisory Council. (2016). Understanding the Costs of Cybercrime. Retrieved from: https://assets.publishing.service.gov.uk/government/uploads/system/uploads/attachment_data/file/674046/understanding-costs-of-cyber-crime-horr96.pdf

8 Morgan, S. (2019). 2019 Official Annual Cybercrime Report. Retrieved from: https://www.herjavecgroup.com/wp-content/uploads/2018/12/CV-HG-2019-Official-Annual-Cybercrime-Report.pdf

9 Whitman, E. M. & Mattord, J. H. (2017). *Management of Information Security* (5th Ed). Cengage Learning, Boston, MA, p. 70.

10 Whitman, E. M. & Mattord, J. H. (2017). *Management of Information Security* (5th Ed). Cengage Learning, Boston, MA.

2

GLOBAL CYBERCRIME

Learning Objectives

- Gain clarity on cybercrime and its impact on the world.
- Gain knowledge of the type of cybercrimes being committed worldwide.
- Comprehend why cybersecurity policy and laws are essential.

"According to McAfee's 2008 Virtual Criminology Report, there are over 120 nations "leveraging the Internet for political, military, and economic espionage activities".[1] Thus, to effectively impose cybersecurity public policy that enacts citizen Internet usage governance, worthy of respect and voluntary adherence, requires gaining understanding about what is manifesting globally in cybercrime. Cybercrime has a long-standing history that continues being just as powerful today, as it was when the first cybercrime was recorded in the United States. In fact, in 1981, Ian Murphy was recorded as the first person found guilty of a cybercrime, resulting from his successful hack of an American telephone company to manipulate its internal clock, so users of the clock could make free calls at peak times. The result of this criminal case evoked United States Congress to pass a Bill into law classified as the Comprehensive Control Crime Act, addressing the unauthorized access and use of computers and computer networks. Then in 1986, the United States Congress enacted the Computer Fraud and Abuse Act, which helped modify the initial statue 18. U.S.C. § 1030.

However, cybercrimes committed outside the United States often cannot be prosecuted or penalized under the United States Computer Fraud and Abuse Act, if the cybercriminal is not conducting crimes under the United States jurisdiction. Thus, with this knowledge readily available to cybercriminals online, in many

DOI: 10.1201/9781003259145-3

instances, prosecuting cybercriminals for crimes conducted via the Internet is not often easy to do with current cybersecurity policy and legal regulatory models. This impacts the ability to effectively decrease the growing rate of cybercrimes occurring globally. In fact, research compiled from The United States Council of Economic Advisors in February 2018, convey that "malicious cyber activity cost the U.S. economy between $57 billion and $109 billion in 2016".[2] Furthermore, both the government and industry sources convey that, "malicious cyber activity is a growing concern for both the public and private sectors. Between 2013 and 2015, according to the Office of the Director of National Intelligence (DNI), cyber threats were the most important strategic threat facing the United States" (see note 2 Ibid).

Additional reports convey that most cybercrimes conducted towards the United States derive from Russia, China, Iran, and North Korea. This is challenging to understand; after all, why would any country government willingly declare to join forces to build their economy with the United States, if that same government supports the nefarious actions of cybercriminals inhabiting their terrain?

In fact, the Netherlands shared in their 2018–2022 cybersecurity public policy that "in various international policy arenas, the role of the US as a leader is changing, while other traditional major powers like Russia and China are becoming more assertive."[3] Thus, to merge cybersecurity public policy models deployed globally, the Council of Europe's Cybercrime Convention presented the idea of establishing a treaty that can govern cybercrime and enable all countries and nation states to effectively implement laws and policy that help protect each country and nation state members from cybercrimes deployed against public sector information systems and all private sector operating in partnership with public sector entities. Doing so will create "a common criminal policy aimed at the protection of society against cybercrime."[4] It also would require signatories to willfully adopt legislation efforts to classify specific computer crimes, including crimes relating to illegal access and interception, data and information system interference, malicious use of devices, forgery, fraud, child pornography, and unauthorized use of intellectual property. Furthermore, it must enforce countries to adopt international laws to effectively investigate computer-related crimes and provide the cooperation all countries and nation state members need to effectively prosecute cybercriminals within other countries and nation states, including supporting extradition of cybercriminals who violate international cybercrime laws and cybersecurity public policy.

Even if such an agreement could be agreed upon, many public and private sector groups and individuals still believe such a union of cybercrime defense would be unsuccessful in decreasing the growing number of cybercrimes conducted globally. After all, civil suits have been filed in federal courts arising from known facts regarding the support ISPs (Internet Service Providers) are rendering at cost, to end-users, to conduct and engage in cybercrimes globally. So, while issues and concerns evolve around cybercrime laws and cybersecurity public policy; the power Internet Service Providers embody, plays a significant role in how government can enact laws and establish cybersecurity public policy, to decrease and control cybercrime. However, until an agreement is established with all governments, Parliaments, and Ministries, responsible for protecting information systems and citizen's data and privacy rights, there remains an open highway for cybercriminals to engage in and get away with billions of dollars and not be prosecuted or held accountable.

Thus, the biggest loophole in deriving at an agreement towards an international cybercrime law encompasses indifferences of cultural language and interpretation of what many believe violates criminal laws enveloping cybercrime. To overcome this stagnation of clarity and language barrier requires all countries and nation state governments, Parliaments, and Ministries to improve their degree of respect towards each country and nation state cybersecurity public policy and Internet crime laws. Achieving this hurdle of acceptance is not easy. After all, evidence supports misunderstanding in tones of speech and facial expressions expressed during communication, dating back to World War I. Next, there are issues with translation of languages (e.g., German into English, etc.). There are also concerns regarding the rights of governments to establish their own approach to conducting surveillance on their citizens; particularly, in matters of national security. Thus, there must be an agreement between all parties involved to establish an international cybercrime law and cybersecurity public policy, everyone will respect and rely on as the primary framework for all stakeholders to implement, without the burden of violating international criminal law ethics in cybercriminal investigation and prosecution.

Another issue blocking the establishment of reaching an international cybercrime law also is enveloped in adherence and respect from all signatories. Countries have been at odds for centuries regarding the lack of respect deployed towards one another for various reasons, that often are outdated and have no relevance to the current trends in what is manifesting in society today. Even worse, research conveys that many countries and nation state governments are actively involved in conducting cyber warfare, cyber terrorism, cyber espionage, and supporting cybercriminals within their jurisdiction. In fact, research conveys that in 2008, Israel launched Operation Cast Lead against Palestine. "A corresponding cyber war quickly erupted between Israeli and Arabic hackers, which has been the norm of late when two nation-states are at war."[5]

In 2017, one of the world's most disruptive cyberattacks occurred under the classification Wanna Cry Ransomware. This malicious software attack locked up files on more than 100 countries information systems, including the cancellation of more than 20,000 hospital appointments in the United Kingdom. Companies such as car manufacturer Renault and international shipping service provider FedEx were crippled and lost millions in revenue earnings. While the attacks were attributed to North Korea; seemingly, there were not many, if at all, prosecuted for the cybercrimes committed in this catastrophic attack.

Even worse, cyber espionage is seen as being far more pervasive than cyber warfare, and the leading nation that is reported as the worse actor of such criminal activity, is the People's Republic of China. Accusations about China's involvement in willfully committed cybercrimes against the United States and nation state members date back to 2002, when the United States Department of Defense reported that "China had downloaded 10 to 20 terabytes of data from the NIPR-Net (DOD's Non-Classified IP Router Network)."[6] Therefore, overcoming such accusations and building trust in each country or nation state member, is not something foreseeably happening overnight. After all, past wars still resonate with many countries and nation state members, who have been at war or victims of such, based on the actions and misinterpretation of information, shared, and disseminated by their ancestry. Their ancestry was not as knowledgeable and/or informed as society is today. Neither did they have access to the Internet as we do today. Today, we have access to global national libraries and universities, and can research facts to gain clarity on all subject matters in milliseconds, with the use of the Internet and computers or mobile devices.

Thus, to establish a framework that is universally respected requires a union of faith in trusting that all countries and nation state members, agree that cybercrime is a threat to the economy and all citizens privacy rights, to engage and communicate with family, friends, and business partners, while respecting and adhering to the cybersecurity public policy and laws enacted worldwide. In fact, the International Telecommunication Union in alignment with government public policy, oversees matters encompassing cybersecurity, and strongly believe, their role is to support establishing trust and "building confidence and security in the use of Information and Communication Technologies". Their model of building confidence and security in the use of Information and Communication Technologies was established in 2001 and have continued improving annually. "At the September 2009 SG17 meeting, several significant, if not historical actions were taken to bring about substantially enhanced global cybersecurity. These actions included the adoption of a Cybersecurity Information Exchange Techniques (CYBEX) initiative that imports more than twenty "best of breeds" standards for platforms developed over the past several years by government agencies and industry to enhance cybersecurity and infrastructure protection."[7] In 2015, the first known structured ontology for cybersecurity information exchange was produced by Japan's NICT research center.

Today, the International Telecommunication Union provides access to data encompassing cybersecurity matters through its online Global Cybersecurity Index. This index measures the commitment deployed by each country to increase awareness regarding the value of cybersecurity, and to share the various dimensions on this subject matter. With the use of five pillars: legal measures, technical measures, organizational measures, capacity building, and cooperation, the ITU scores how effective and efficient each countries cybersecurity approach is. While this is a dynamic infrastructure to encourage public and private sector to manage their cybersecurity policy, this organization is a private sector entity. Secondary data sources are instrumental in bringing attention to poorly enacted and mismanaged cybersecurity public policy development, implementation, and management. However, each government addressing cybersecurity public policy is responsible for staying current with global trends in cybercrime and updating their cybersecurity public policy annually. However, even when updates are implemented, how can we derive at a conclusion that any nation state member or country cybersecurity public policy is an effective model that will be respected and adhered to; especially when there remains an endless misconception regarding the ethics and integrity each country and nation state member embodies. One way to gain clarity on this subject matter is to understand the cultural and social ethics within each country and nation state.

Cultural and Social Ethics

With religion as the forefront of many citizens environmental conditioning, many governments face the daunting task of better-educating citizens about concerns, they have about their religious teaching and beliefs. After all, in 2017, Pew Research Center shared staggering statistics regarding the current number of religious followers worldwide. This research conveys that 2.3 billion people worldwide are Christian; 1.8 billion are Muslims; 1.2 billion are unaffiliated; 1.1 billion are Hindu; 0.5 billion are Buddhists; 0.4 are Folk religions; 0.1 billion are other religions; and 0.01 billion are Jews.[8] When a society is raised with traditions and beliefs deeply rooted in religion; coming of age does not always mean forgetting what has been embedded in people's hearts and minds. Instead, knowing these facts should make us more concerned about how we can remove the fears and diminish ignorance.

To many, religion is complex. In fact, religion is central to billions of people's lives and has gained influential political significance in today's world. Karl Marx once stated that not only do religions pacify people falsely; religions can become tools of oppression.[9] Furthermore, Mary Pat Fisher explains briefly in her textbook title Living Religions that Psychoanalyst Sigmund Freud (1856–1938) once stated that religions embody collective fantasy. Religious beliefs tend to provide religious followers a God powerful enough to protect them from terrors of life and reward or punish them for obedience or nonobedience to social norms. Fisher explained briefly, in part, that

Freud's extremely skeptical point of view regarding religious belief, can be understood as an illusion rooting from people's infantile insecurities and guilt, and can often mirror mental illness (see Ibid).

Furthermore, Karl Marx is believed to have thought that religion as well as all other components of its social structure-derives from an economic framework.[10] Mary Pat Fisher also explains that religions propose ideals that radically transform people's concepts of reality. To a point that many religious followers believe they can personally communicate with- God- in a heaven like sanctuary defined by man's terminology of such and man's belief systems. To many others who are not in alignment with such ideology; this is absurd and irrational thinking. Nevertheless, these concepts of thought and belief drive the mental and emotional state of billions of religious followers worldwide, who cling to religion as a safeguard that empowers them to live a life of happiness and security without fear of being victims of cyber warfare or cyberattacks.

Many nation state members and countries laws are designed and infused with their traditional religious teaching and beliefs. So much, in some Islamic or Muslim countries, women are secondary to men, and there is no second-guessing this tradition. This derives from religious teaching that was deeply rooted in the traditions of those countries, and no external country or nation state is given power to diminish or discredit the beliefs within such societies. Thus, those countries that enact the rights of its citizens to conduct nefarious acts against nation states and countries, in the name of their religions, are not going to relinquish their traditions simply to meet the needs of countries and nation states, to decrease or deter cyberattacks or cybercrimes.

To such persons, that is their traditional right to defend their belief system in alignment with their ancestry teaching. Despite if such beliefs are right or wrong, ethical or unethical, true or false. To build bridges that will be effective in thwarting cybercrime globally requires possessing knowledge on religion and how this entity controls and impacts the decision of law makers and policy makers in those countries and nation states that are governed by religious beliefs and traditions.

Thus, the war against cybercriminals and cybercrime is a war that deserves serious research and consideration of all facts and issues; for any cybercriminal laws or cybersecurity public policy to have an impact on decreasing cybercrime. In fact, when researching 43 countries and their cybercrime statistics, the following information was discovered:

- In **Afghanistan**, where Islam is the primary religion; an upsurge of cybercrime and electronic crimes surfaced in 2009, evoking the need for the Afghanistan government to design and implement its first cybersecurity strategy. Today, the Afghanistan government thrives to "protect and assure data, information and IT infrastructure security in Afghanistan's cyberspace, enhance capacities to prevent and response to cyber threats, protect the children and youth of Afghanistan in cyberspace, mitigate the risk of vulnerability, prevent damage from cyber threats and incidents through a variety of standardized institutional structures, policies, procedures, people, technologies, and administrative processes."[11]
- In **Australia**, Christianity is the primary religion. Cybercrimes commonly committed include computer intrusion, unauthorized modification of data, destruction of data, denial of service attacks, malicious software, financial fraud, and child pornography.
- In **Bermuda**, Catholicism is the primary religion; increased cybercrime relating to email fraud and telecommunication phone calls posing as computer technicians requesting access to personal computer and/or business computers with remote access are on the rise. According to Bermuda government in its 2018–2022 Cybersecurity Strategy, cybercriminals steal personal information and utilize Ransomware and additional malware to extort money from businesses and individuals.
- In **Canada**, Christianity is the primary religion; cybercrimes typically include child pornography, indecent and harassing communications, and uttering threats. The Canada government conveys in its Cybersecurity Strategy that "criminals and other malicious cyber threat actors-many of which operate outside our borders-take advantage of security gaps, low cyber security awareness, and technological developments to compromise cyber systems. They steal personal and financial information, intellectual property, and trade secrets."[12]

- In **Chili**, the primary religion is Catholicism. Cybercrimes commonly committed in this nation state include Distributed Denial of Service Attacks (DDoS). As a result, the Chili "government has worked since April 2015 through an Inter-ministerial Committee on Cybersecurity on the development of Chili's first National Cybersecurity Policy, which has been fine-tuned after a successful Citizen Consultation process carried out between February and March 2016."[13]
- In **Croatia**, the primary religion is Catholicism. Cybercrimes commonly practiced in that nation state include unauthorized access, computer system interference, computer data damage, data forgery, computer fraud, misuse of devices, unlawful use of personal data, and exploitation of children for pornography.
- In **Cyprus**, the primary religion is Greek Orthodox. Cyber-crimes commonly committed include email fraud, Ransomware attacks, social media and email account hacking, identity theft, and child pornography.
- In **Czech Republic**, the primary religion is Roman Catholic. Cybercrimes commonly deployed include fake online ecom-merce, phishing attacks, and exploitation of personal data, as well as an increase in Ransomware attacks.
- In **Dubai**, the primary religion is Islam. Cybercrimes com-mitted in 2019 included credential phishing, insider threats, surveillance and hacking, telecommunications, oil and gas sector attacks, including spear phishing.
- In **Egypt**, the primary religion is Islam. Cybercrimes com-monly launched in 2019 included identity theft, attacking public and private Web sites, dissemination of fake news tar-geting national security.
- In **Estonia**, the primary religion is Unaffiliated, Eastern Orthodox, Lutheran, and Protestant. Cybercrimes commonly deployed include Ransomware attacks, narcotics trade, and money laundering.
- In **European Union**, the primary religion is Christianity. Cybercrimes commonly practiced include child pornography, payment card fraud, child sexual abuse, Crime-as-a-Service business, and extortion. Often utilized are botnets infused with malware, fake anti-virus software download, money

laundering, sale of weapons, false passports, cloned credit cards, and drugs, as well as hacking services.

- In **Finland**, the primary religion is Christian. Cybercrimes commonly deployed include Denial of Service Attacks, malware attacks, hacking; fraud, money laundering and extortion; child sexual abuse; distribution of propaganda and terrorist material; recruitment of organized crime members, and planning of terrorist attacks.
- In **Gambia**, the primary religion is Muslim. The cybercrimes committed include fake news dissemination, libel and slander, electronic bullying, and electronic eavesdropping.
- In **Germany**, the primary religion is Christianity. Cybercrimes commonly practiced include cybercrime as a service (e.g., hacking services and malicious software installation), Ransomware, and industrial espionage.
- In **Greece**, the primary religion is Greek Orthodox. Cybercrimes commonly practiced include hacking of computer systems, destruction of unauthorized dissemination of software (e.g., digital data and audiovisual material), child pornography, and online harassment (e.g., cyberbullying).
- In **Hungary**, the primary religion is Christianity. Cybercrimes commonly practiced include phishing, malware attacks, DDOS, exploitation of vulnerabilities, unauthorized access of information, and Web site defacement.
- In **Iceland**, the primary religion is Christianity. Cybercrimes committed include child pornography, defamation, cyberbullying, hate crimes, virus attacks on computers, theft or destruction of computerized data, and cyber-espionage.
- In **Italy**, the primary religion is Catholicism. Cybercrimes committed include credit card fraud, ATM skimming, identity hacking, Internet romance and financial scams, SPAM, online dating scams, money transfer, fake business contracts; grandparents/relative targeting, fake Inheritance notices, fake work permits, and fake job offers.
- In **Japan**, the primary religion is Shinto. Cybercrimes commonly committed include Malware and viruses, accessing computers without authorization, illegal access to trade secrets, identity theft, fraud, and phishing.

- In **Kenya**, the primary religions are Christianity and Islam. Cybercrimes commonly committed include forgery, child pornography, unauthorized access and damage to computer devices, access with intent to commit offenses, unauthorized modification of computer data, unauthorized and access to computer services, system interference, and misuse of devices.
- In **Kosovo**, the primary religion is unknown, although a significant number of citizens are Muslim. Cybercrimes commonly committed include Distributed Denial of Service Attacks (DDOSA), online radicalization, cyberbullying, fake news, and exploitation of vulnerabilities.
- In **Kuwait**, the primary religion is Islam. Cybercrimes commonly committed include hacking, information theft, privacy violations, money laundering, extortion, drug dealing, arms smuggling, human trafficking, child abuse, and financial manipulation. Cyber espionage and defamation are also committed online. Furthermore, Malware attacks, DDOSA, piracy of personal data, SPAM, identity theft, and unauthorized access of computers.
- In **Luxemburg**, the primary religion is Roman Catholicism. Commonly committed cybercrimes include Malware attacks, stealing passwords, creating botnets, trade hacking, money laundering, online fraud, child sexual exploitation, sale of weapons, false passports, counterfeit and cloned credit cards, and illegal drug sales.
- In **Malaysia**, the primary religion is Islam. Cybercrimes include unauthorized intrusion, Web defacement, harassment, destruction of computers, denial of service attacks, fraud, forgery, phishing scams, mailbombs, and copyright piracy.
- In **Nepal**, the primary religion is Hinduism. Cybercrimes commonly committed include ATM attacks, Pos Attacks, DDOSA, Ransomware, spear phishing, data breaching, and fake news. Piracy, destroying or altering computer code, unauthorized access to computer materials, damaging computer information systems, computer fraud, and publishing illegal materials in electronic form are also committed.
- In the **Netherlands**, the primary religion is Roman Catholic. Cybercrimes commonly committed include phishing, identity

theft, hacking, hate crimes, misuse of Web sites and computer networks, child pornography, and sexual advances to minors.

- In **New Zealand**, the primary religion is Christian and Hindu. Cybercrimes committed include computer intrusion, SQL attacks, cross-site scripting, man-in-the-middle attacks, Malware attacks, DDOSA attacks. Online scams, child pornography, and identity theft.

- In **Norway**, the primary religion is Lutheran Christianity. Cybercrimes commonly committed are computer hacking, theft and fraud; child exploitation, cyberbullying, and hate crimes.

- In **Poland**, the primary religions are Islam, Judaism, Hinduism, and Buddhism. The cybercrimes commonly committed include SPAM, hate crimes, piracy, child pornography, child sexual abuse, fraud, and identity theft.

- In **Rwanda**, the primary religion is Christianity. Cybercrimes commonly committed include fraud, money laundering, identity theft, bank PIN code fraud, job fraud, counterfeit titles, and real estate fraud.

- In **Samoa**, the primary religion is Christianity. Cybercrimes commonly committed remain low in this country.

- In **Singapore**, the primary religions are Buddhism, Hinduism, Islam, Christianity, Sikhism, Jainism, and Judaism. Cybercrimes commonly committed include hacking, credit card fraud, e-commerce fraud, fake job and payment fees, Ransomware and Malware attacks; online dating scams, Web site defacement, COVID-19 phishing scams, and Internet of Things attacks.

- In **Slovakia**, the primary religions are Catholicism and Protestant. Cybercrimes commonly committed include credit card fraud, stalking, defamation, false accusations, extortion, Malware, spear phishing, and cyber-espionage.

- In **South Africa**, the primary religions are Christianity, Islam, Hinduism, Buddhism, and Judaism. Cybercrimes commonly committed include Ransomware, hacking, identity theft, phishing scams, electronic funds transfer fraud, child pornography, cyberbullying, cyber-impersonation, and social media profile cloning.

- In **Switzerland**, the primary religion is Christianity. Cybercrimes commonly committed include hacking, stealing personal data, extortion, SPAM, phishing emails, e-banking Malware, payment methods and outstanding invoices, fake invoices, fake advertisement, online auctions, classified advertising Web sites, and real estate fraud.

- In **Thailand**, the primary religion is Buddhism. Cybercrimes commonly committed include AI hacking, phishing, identity theft, theft and sale of corporate data, hacking, cyber extortion, and cyber espionage.
- In **Trinidad and Tobago**, the primary religion is Baha'i' Faith, Christian, Islam, Roman Catholic, Hindu, and Muslim. Cybercrimes commonly committed include online harassment, cyberbullying, defamation of character, phishing, celebrity name misuse, fake accounts, and social media fake account creation.
- In **Uganda**, the primary religions are Islam, Christianity, and Roman Catholic. The common cybercrimes include email and Web site scams (e.g., fake Visas and free transportation).
- In the **United Arab Emirates**, the primary religion is Islam. Cybercrimes commonly committed include Cyber blackmailing, money laundering, identity theft, fraud, hacking, and theft of financial assets and data.
- In the **United Kingdom**, the primary religion is Christianity, Islam, Hinduism, Sikhism, Judaism, and Buddhism. Cybercrimes commonly committed include hacking, malicious software, DDOSA (Distributed Denials of Service Attacks), trolling, revenge porn, cyberbullying, child sexual exploitation, online stalking, and virtual mobbing.
- In **Vietnam**, the primary religions are Folk Religion/Atheism, Buddhism, Christianity, and Catholicism. Cybercrimes commonly committed include hacking, bank fraud, credit card skimming, and phishing.

As conveyed in this chapter, cybercrimes committed globally often include hacking as the primary gateway to gain unauthorized access to computer devices and mobile phones. Unfortunately, global technology end-users continue neglecting to adhere to government recommendations and guidelines regarding the best methods to practice and deploy, to protect technology tools and information assets. Since these tools provide a bridge to gain unauthorized access to computer systems, devices, and mobile phones, cybercriminals prey on the ignorance of end-users. This gateway of access enables cybercrime to soar.

Furthermore, while many governments and nation state members continue attempting to establish cybersecurity public policy and National Security Information Security Policy, global citizens continue working closely with private sector service providers (e.g., ISPs), who are commonly known for aiding cybercriminals in their quest to gain access to citizens personal data and technology devices. In fact, Maine enacted a law in 2019, An Act to Protect the Privacy of Online Customer Information (LD 946, to be codified at 35-AM.R.S.c. 94), which prohibits Internet Service Providers from utilizing, disclosing, selling, or permitting access to consumers information generated by a consumer's usage of an Internet Service Provider. This law is one attempt deployed to provide consumers in Maine the assurance that their government is taking the steps to enact laws and policy that protect their right to privacy and their access and usage of Internet services.

Unfortunately, Internet Service Providers violate consumer's privacy by compiling records of consumers Web site and internet usage history, geographical location data, text messages, and more. This invasion of privacy does not coexist with federal laws regarding Electronic Communication Act, and establishes a degree of distrust, while violating consumer's rights. Thus, cybercriminals can gain access to this data and build partnerships with Internet Service Providers to gain access to consumer's computers and mobile devices and deploy cyberattacks without being named culprits. This nefarious act of abuse of authority often goes unprosecuted because common consumers believe, they are protected and their usage of mobile devices and computer systems, remain secure.

To improve these issues of concern, governments should continue working diligently to establish an international communication of legal authority that bridges the gap of legal authorization, to enact laws and penalties for violators who engage in nefarious cybercrimes, including Internet Service Providers. After all, cybercrime is costing countries and nation states billions in losses annually. In fact, the loss of economic stability in many countries over the last ten years, equates to more than $100 trillion. This loss of economic gain impacts the ability for government to provide citizens the services needed to live their lives free of oppression and poverty. Unless things change and more emphasis is deployed towards securing nation states and countries, Internet highways, and end-users' online engagement. Cybercriminals will continue making more money than public and private sector and invoke more citizens to engage in such activities; instead of partnering with their government to stamp out this wickedness.

Summary

Cybercrime continues manifesting around the globe, impacting economies and defeating laws and overruling policies. While government, Parliaments, and Ministries grapple for answers to decrease this war of organized crime syndicate greed; consumers remain nonchalant in their efforts to protect themselves from victimization of cybercrime and cybercriminals. This ignorance and seemingly nonchalant attitude continue enabling cybercrime to increase, and cost countries and nation state members, trillions in losses annually. Unless serious efforts are made to combat this spread of crime, many nation states and countries face the daunting task of winning a war on cybercrime that has no immediate end.

Establishing cybersecurity public policy is one way to enable public and private sector to build stronger alliances and partnerships that can infuse a better union of engagement that helps protect public and private sector partnerships. However, when the culprit commonly relied upon for Internet services plays a role in deploying cybercrimes. Governments continue being victimized themselves. Take, for instance, the Center for Strategic & International Studies shared details regarding cyberattack incidents conducted in 2020. Incidence included a November 2020 attack which, "Hamas used a secret headquarter in Turkey to carry out cyberattacks and counterintelligence."[14]

In October 2020, the United States government shared news that Iranian hackers were attempting to hack election Web sites. This incident resulted in a spokesperson from China's Foreign Ministry to declare the United States is an "empire of hacking". Furthermore, India shared news that cybercrimes against its government was more than $16 billion. And a Russian cyber-espionage group successfully hacked into the European government organizational Web site.

These incidents are not the tip of the iceberg. In fact, in 2019, the Office of the Director of National Intelligence for the United

States of America shared the Statement for the Record Worldwide Threat Assessment of the US Intelligence Community. This publicly shared data conveys that technology is a growing asset to the growth and sustainability of the United States of America and continues to be the bridge that enables our economy to grow and provide U.S. citizens economic independence. Yet due to the continued disregard for U.S. National Security laws and cybersecurity public policy. The United States remains vulnerable to cyberattacks that include cyber espionage. Thus, efforts to protect the nation's information system are under way and must be the priority of the intelligence agencies to assure Americans that our information systems are secure and non-impenetrable.

Even though such efforts are being implemented. Adversaries such as North Korea, Russia, Syria, and ISIS, are utilizing chemical weapons (e.g., nerve agents and toxic industrial chemicals) as methods to become more diverse in their attack models. With the increased usage of technology and Malware attacks, these adversaries can overcome efforts implemented by the United States government, if the United States does not increase its education and training efforts to select citizens to become protection agents in the war against cybercrime. Furthermore, with the use of satellites, such as Russia Sputnik, and others alike. It is likely that these technology tools will soon become gateways of attacking Americans and nation state members, who are not tech knowledgeable and savvy to thwart against such evil methods of attack. If one of our adversaries were to gain access to controlling such a satellite model that could very well launch laser attacks and penetrate citizen's mobile devices or computers while citizens are talking and engaging on their devices. The impact could be catastrophic and more powerful than COVID-19.

Thus, the best model to implement is developing effective cybersecurity public policy that can be instrumental models for private sector to integrate within, their cybersecurity and information system framework. Yet to achieve this goal requires private sector to relinquish their fear of being surveillance by the United States government, who seeks to protect citizen's right to privacy and their ability to reach their economic growth goals. When governments share interest in protecting their citizens' rights to utilize the Internet for their professional and personal growth; citizens must work in concert with government. Going forward in this book, you will gain knowledge on what 43 countries are doing to protect and educate citizens about cybercrime and cybersecurity public policy. To safeguard the very information systems, we rely on, we must begin to respect the decisions implemented by our government, and trust that these professionals are doing their best and going beyond to protect and serve our needs pertaining to Internet privacy rights and information system usage, storage, and transmission of sensitive data.

"We need increasing deterrence in cyberspace."

– Army Lt. General Paul Nakasone

Discussion Questions

1. How many nations are leveraging the Internet for political, military, and economic espionage activities?
2. Who was recorded as the first person found guilty of a cybercrime?
3. How much has malicious cybercrime activity cost the U.S. economy?
4. What countries primarily are held accountable for conducting cybercrime towards the United States?
5. Who presented the idea of establishing a treaty?
6. What is the biggest loophole in reaching an agreement towards an international cybercrime law?
7. How many people make religion central in their lives?
8. What author believed that a cultures religion derives from its economic framework?

Case Study

The greatest threat to any company in the world is cybercrime. Its therefore a global issue of concern and one of the biggest and complex problems with mankind. For instance, in 2016, cybersecurity cybercrime cost the world $6 trillion annually and by 2023 its predicted to be up by $10 trillion or more. This is more profitable than the global trade of major illegal drugs combined. Thus, cybercrime must be fought globally.

SCENARIO: A Department of Health supervisor left their work-issued unencrypted laptop, which had access to over 50,000 medical records, in a locked department car while running to use a bathroom in a retail store. The laptop was stolen after the car was broken into. What might happen and what policy should be put in place?

Based on what you have read in this chapter, what will be the average cost of cybercrime in the 43 countries discussed, and why?

Notes

1 Carr, J. (2012). *Inside Cyber Warfare* (2nd Ed). O'Reilly Media, Inc., Sebastopol, CA, p. 1.

2 Council of Economic Advisors. (2018). The Cost of Malicious Cyber Activity to the U.S. Economy. Retrieved from: https://www.whitehouse.gov/wp-content/uploads/2018/03/The-Cost-of-Malicious-Cyber-Activity-to-the-U.S.-Economy.pdf

3 Ministry of Foreign Affairs. (2018). Working Worldwide for the Security of Netherlands. Retrieved from: https://www.government.nl/documents/reports/2018/05/14/integrated-international-security-strategy-2018-2022

4 Council of Europe. (2014). Convention on Cybercrime. Retrieved from: https://www.coe.int/en/web/conventions/full-list/-/conventions/treaty/185

5 Carr, J. (2012). *Inside Cyber Warfare* (2nd Ed). O'Reilly Media, Inc., Sebastopol, CA, p. 1.

6 Carr, J. (2012). *Inside Cyber Warfare* (2nd Ed). O'Reilly Media, Inc., Sebastopol, CA, p. 4.

7 ITU.int. (2020). ITU Cybersecurity Activities. Retrieved from: https://www.itu.int/en/action/cybersecurity/Pages/default.aspx

8 Hackett, C. & McClendon, D. (2017). Pew Research Center: Fact Tank News in the Numbers. Retrieved from: https://www.pewresearch.org/fact-tank/2017/04/05/christians-remain-worlds-largest-religious-group-but-they-are-declining-in-europe/

9 Fisher, P. M. (2008). *Living Religions* (7th Ed). Pearson Education, Inc., Upper Saddle River, NJ, p. 3.

10 Fisher, P. M. (2008). *Living Religions* (7th Ed). Pearson Education, Inc., Upper Saddle River, NJ.

11 Islamic Republic of Afghanistan Ministry of Communication and IT. (2014). National Cyber Security Strategy of Afghanistan. Retrieved from: http://nic.af/Content/files/National%20Cybersecurity%20Strategy%20of%20Afghanistan%20(November2014).pdf

12 Canada National Security Strategy. (2018). Retrieved from: https://www.publicsafety.gc.ca/cnt/rsrcs/pblctns/ntnl-cbr-scrt-strtg/index-en.aspx

13 Chili National Cybersecurity Policy. (2017). Mahmud Aleuy PeÑa y Lillo. Retrieved from: https://www.ciberseguridad.gob.cl/media/2017/05/NCSP-ENG.pdf

14 Center for Strategic & International Studies. (2020). Significant Cyber Incidents. Retrieved from: https://www.csis.org/programs/strategic-technologies-program/significant-cyber-incidents

3

DIPLOMACY IN INTERNET POLICY

Learning Objectives

- Understand why diplomacy in Internet policy is essential.
- Gain knowledge of steps deployed to integrate diplomacy in cybersecurity policy.
- Learn about organizations who impact diplomacy in cybersecurity policy.
- Learn what countries are doing to infuse Internet policy.

Self-expression is an inalienable right encompassed within the liberties bestowed unto citizens in a democratic society. This inalienable right includes the ability to utilize technology and all hardware and software applications integrated in such, to develop, implement, and manage whatever creative art, music, document, or information, an individual desires to share, store, and transmit, with the use of technology and the Internet globally. Yet too often many disregard the inalienable rights of others, assuming everyone does not deserve to have the right to express themselves open and freely. Instead, such persons believe those that do not think, act, or live as they do, should be oppressed and denied the right to be free to express their ideology. To help shed light on this barbaric form of oppression and residential imprisonment, global public and private sector are taking the initiative to define public policy and laws to protect citizens rights and keep them safe and secure from harm, particularly while surfing the Internet.

In fact, the European Union developed the Online Privacy Law to render protection for citizens in the United States of America, as well as all EU Member States. This law was brought to attention in 2012, to reform existing legislative framework and to bridge the gap between member states, in deploying a structured law that protects the rights

DOI: 10.1201/9781003259145-4

of citizens to utilize technology and the Internet, for their personal and business use and prosperity, without fear and without victimization. This law is available for citizen research and clarity on the United States Library of Congress Web site under the title: *Online Privacy Law: European Union*, and outlines the steps taken by European Court of Justice, in May 2014, to update this law and include Directive 95/46/EC, which focuses on the "fundamental principles on the processing of personal data".[1] Under this law, citizens have the right to take an active role in determining how public and private sector utilizes, their personal data. This includes controlling how their data is stored, shared, and retrieved through collaborative usage of public and private sector software applications and database information systems. This law provides additional layers of security for matters regarding citizens: race, ethnic origin, political affiliations, religion, genetic data, and criminal history. Additionally, this law provides citizens the right to be forgotten. Under the Right to be Forgotten, personal information must be erased immediately wherever the data is no longer required for its original processing purpose, or the data subject has withdrawn his/her consent and there is no other legal ground for processing the data subject has objected to and there are no overriding legitimate grounds for the processing, or erasure is required to fulfill a statutory obligation under the EU law or the right of the Member States.[2]

Unfortunately, while many EU nation member states agree to comply with the laws and policy enacted by government, in many other countries where religion dictates the rights of citizens freedoms (e.g., Islamic states and some Christian countries), even the European Union law remains ignored and inefficient to protect citizens from being victimized by cyberattacks deployed by religious groups, organizations, governments, corporations, individuals, and law enforcement agencies. In fact, many individuals use their religious beliefs, traditions, and practices as tools to hinder citizen's freedom with the use of technology and the Internet. Despite the laws enacted globally to enact citizen's right to democracy, oddly, the war raging around the world continues facing the battle through technology engulfed in cyber warfare and cyber-terrorism.

Thus, if laws are not the gateway to deploy citizen democracy, what will it take to gain respect for a global way of freedom? After all, each country has established its own government to help regulate its citizens and deploy protective methods to assure all citizens the right to feel safe in their person and their affects. When anyone attempts to discredit this democracy, we all suffer. No matter our geographical location in the world, we each thrive to live a life free from oppression and without regulations that hinder our ability to live our best life. This includes having the right to rely on technology and the Internet to engage with family, friends, and peers, without being denied access to all software applications enabling us to effectively communicate. Now that we rely on software applications such as Zoom, Go to Meeting, Microsoft Meetings, Slack, UberConference, and Skype, to communicate globally; citizens are being victimized and targeted by cybercriminals, who access these applications due to the numerous vulnerabilities associated with each software application. Thus, for any country's cybersecurity public policy to be effective requires conducting research on all laws and public policy currently enacted globally, governing the use of any technology component relied upon for both public and private sector. Doing so enables the ability to revise current cybersecurity public policy that may be outdated and not current with the trends of threat and vulnerabilities engulfing technology tools, information systems, information technology, virtual cloud environments, software, hardware, artificial intelligence, Internet of Things, 3D printing, and quantum computing.

Unfortunately, global laws governing the use of the Internet and technology are minimum. Due to this, there are many industry associations and organizations being established to help governments gain a broader scope of clarity on what must be done to keep citizens safe and secure while using the Internet and new technology. Take, for instance, the Internet Engineering Task Force (IETF), which encompasses international designers, operators, vendors, and researchers, are concerned with the evolution of the Internet architecture and the ability for the Internet to operate without end-users being victimized, while utilizing this global gateway of communication sharing. This organization offers an open membership defined by industry categories (e.g., routers, servers, transport, security, etc.). Also included are Area Directors who are members of the Internet Engineering Steering Group. There is also the Internet Society, which encompasses global members who have the same focus of defending the Internet and making it a safe gateway for everyone to utilize.

However, across the globe, governments are wrestling to keep up with the pace of Internet software application development. Thus, there remains a need to implement increased forms of governance.

This results in laws being enacted that focuses on various components of the Internet and technology tools. For instance, in the United States several laws have been passed, including The Electronic Communications Privacy Act, which was enacted in 1986; giving government the ability to access digital communication including email, social media messages, information on public cloud databases, with and in some instance, without the use of a subpoena. This law also enables government to gain access to these components up-to and beyond 180 days, without a warrant. There is also the Computer Fraud and Abuse Act, enacted in the 1980s, which has been modified several times (e.g., 1989, 1994, 1996, and 2001). Additionally, are the Cyber Intelligence Sharing and Protection Act, enacted in 2011 and reintroduced in 2015, as well as the Children's Online Privacy Protection Act that was passed in 2000 and updated in 2013.

While these laws have been enacted to deploy security and make a safe way for Internet usage; there remains a gap in understanding how these laws actually serve to protect all American citizens who access and utilize the Internet. After all, many cybercriminals conduct cyberattacks abroad in territories that are not held accountable to the laws enacted by the United States. As a result, many Americans continue being harassed and attacked online while using the Internet, and often cannot file legal complaints to resolves such matters. In other countries, such as the United Kingdom, where the Retention Data law was passed and is now enveloped under the Investigatory Powers Act of 2016, encompasses the Data Protection Bill. This law provides citizens protection regarding unlawful interception of communication data. Furthermore, the European Court of Justice passed a law rendering protection for citizens' mobile and Internet data usage.

In addition, India passed a law regarding Internet Censorship. In fact, the OpenNet Initiative Report was established in 2011, to deploy a safe and secure Internet experience for citizens, without impeding upon their democracy and civil rights. And in 2008, the Information Technology Act was enacted, which provides framework to regulate access to the Internet and e-commerce. This act enables law enforcement to conduct search and seizure without warrant if probable cause exists in a criminal investigation.

In Africa states such as Algeria, Angola, Botswana, Burkina Faso, Burundi, Cameroon, Central Africa Republic, Chad, Congo, Egypt,

Ethiopia, Gambia, Ghana, Guinea, Ivory Coast, Kenya, Liberia, Libya, Madagascar, Malawi Morocco, Namibia, South Africa, Somalia, Sudan, Tanzania, Togo, Zambia, and Zimbabwe, laws regarding Internet censorship and surveillance have been enacted. While some of these laws may be enacted to protect citizens, many laws are passed to allow government to maintain control over the usage citizen's practice on the Internet within these territories.

For instance, The Post and Telecommunications Act passed in Zimbabwe enables the government to access and retrieve citizen's emails at their own discretion. Citizens can be arrested and penalized for disseminating defamatory information about their government and country. Fines can reach up to $200,000. In Libya, Internet censorship enables the government to block access to pornography, as well as political Web sites belonging to rival groups of political parties. In Angola, citizens are protected from oppression under the Freedom of the Net law, which does not prohibit the use of the Internet or exchange of data.

Although countries seek to stay current with trends in democracy and Internet usage. There remains a broad scope of indifference impeding upon the civil liberties of citizens around the globe, due to political and religious viewpoints of those in authority of many countries. When citizens lack clarity on their rights, the first problem many citizens encounter is subjection to cruel and unusual punishment by authority figures, who too, often lack clarity on their religious beliefs and traditions. Being deprived to utilize the Internet for personal and business affairs by government officials is oppressive and a daunting task to combat if you lack the technology skills to do so.

In China, citizens have been deprived of utilizing the Internet to gain access to social media Web site Facebook. In fact, North Korea, Iran, and Syria also block citizen's access to Facebook. Additionally, citizens in Bangladesh have experienced loss of Facebook temporarily, but are not able to access Twitter. And in, North Korea, citizens cannot access YouTube, Facebook, or Twitter at all.

When a government steps in and enact laws to prohibit citizens from gaining access to vital research, resources, and business opportunities, what is that government expressing to its citizens. After all, citizens help establish the framework for government to exist within most countries. We the People established the government and maintain the daily operation of that government. When We the People lose control over our governance of actions, we are living in an oppressed society.

Thus, to reach a level of equality globally that can be unified and implemented in a democratic and diplomatic approach, citizens must ban together and gain clarity on the issues that matter to them most, regarding technology and the Internet. This requires citizens to become better informed and educated about the facts. Not just conducting research via the Internet, but getting the education needed to take on roles in government to make changes where change are needed. How do you think your government is authorized to make laws and enforce such laws? We vote in America to decide who is qualified to be our leaders. However, our leaders are also our peers. Today, many of our peers are government officials, who live normal lives as we do. The issue arises when we neglect to take the initiative to be leaders in our own lives. Instead, we render control over to our peers, who dictate what we can and cannot do.

The Internet was designed so all citizens around the world could have access to a gateway of communication. We can utilize this medium to share our thoughts, secrets, creative arts, music; complete education courses and degree studies; bank, vote, and engage in Internet teleconference with our physicians. For many societies, there has been a long wanting for a medium that enables all people to excel without control. The Internet and the technology tools integrated within are our resources to explore the world we live in. When access controls are implemented to prevent us from connecting, we are limited and often discouraged from seeking outlets to unleash us from the boundaries, we find ourselves in.

It is only when all governments are working in alignment to defend our needs and consider our rights and freedom to express ourselves, can we be free to engage and enjoy the Internet as it was initially intended to be. Otherwise, we are imprisoned with illusions that cannot be made physical to enjoy, because our scope of clarity is limited. Integrating diplomacy in Internet policy, must provide citizens the right to express their creative selves and share their knowledge, wisdom, research, and life experiences in an open forum of discussion. However, to achieve this goal requires everyone to remain compliant with their country Internet laws and public policy, and avoid violating these decrees, or face the consequences of their actions.

We cannot expect transparency in our government Internet laws and public policy when there are threats associated with utilizing technology tools developed by software developers, who desire to spy on citizens and invade their privacy. Over the last ten years, Internet Service Providers (ISP) have been entangled in federal criminal investigations and civil suits around the globe. In fact, the largest resource that enables an open gateway to citizen's privacy via the Internet, computer, or mobile devices, are Internet Service Providers (ISP). "In 1995, commercial Internet Service Providers (ISPs) took over the backbone of the Internet. They also became the on-ramp to the Internet. Anyone wanting to use the Internet must go through an ISP".[3]

Today, research convey that internet activity is monitored by an Internet Service Provider (ISP) and can be hijacked. While there is little consumers can do about attacks at the ISP level, the Web pages, you visit can also be tracked by cookies, which are small bits of text that are downloaded and stored by your browser. Browser plugins may also track your activity across multiple Web sites.[4] Thus, when governments consider what needs to be assessed in the structure of defining their cybersecurity public policy, it is essential to include elements regarding the security deployed against citizens' privacy in correlation with Internet Service Providers (ISP). However, even then, there remains legal concern that government cannot immediately combat. After all, consumerism allows citizens to make purchasing choices that meet their immediate and long-term needs. Thus, consumers are required to take the initiative to investigate their Internet Service Providers (ISP), to learn how these service providers utilize, collect, store, and share, their data.

This is the double-edge sword that keeps our government and legislatures entangled in legal squabbles regarding the privacy of citizens, how to avoid violating citizens democracy, and develop effective Internet public policy that can protect and secure citizens' rights. While we can always look at things from a negative perspective. We also must embrace the opportunities that embody our government's ability to elect and install Internet laws and public policy, to enable us the freedom to utilize the Internet and technology as we see fit, for whatever purposes we have desire to do so. Unfortunately, we live in a world where everyone is not equal or feel as though they are equal, and tend to utilize the Internet, technology, and Internet Service Providers (ISP) for nefarious reasons that amount to criminal activity and global cybercrime.

In fact, research compiled by the United States Federal Bureau of Investigations reported that in 2019, there were 467,361 complaints, with an average of $3.5 billion in losses to individuals and businesses. Crimes commonly deployed, include phishing and non-payment-non-delivery scams, and extortion. Most crimes committed were business email scams, romance and confidence fraud; spoofing, or mimicking the account of individuals or vendors known for victimizing individuals to collect personal or financial data.[5] Crimes around the globe are much similar. Take, for instance, cybercrimes accounted for 32% of cyberattacks and breaches in the United Kingdom in 2019. Additional reports shared by SPECOPS convey that the Netherlands, Bulgaria, Belarus, Ukraine, Bosnia, Lithuania, Romania, France, Hungary, and Croatia face high cybercrime.[6]

Summary

So, how can governments maintain control over cybercrime and secure the Internet for citizens who rely on commercial Internet Service Providers (ISPs), who spy on consumers and share their data with third-party sources. One way to overcome this issue is joining local cybersecurity associations and organizations email listings to learn about the current trends in cybersecurity and cybercrimes. Doing so will enable you to gain leverage over cybercriminals and better understand how to protect your information assets from strangers. Furthermore, doing so will enable you to become instrumental in sharing your voice and making a difference in the way government enacts cybersecurity public policy and laws in your country. Most importantly, taking the initiative to make change in the way Internet Service Providers (ISPs) respect consumers, will introduce a new approach to how ISPs connect with consumers and respect their privacy rights.

Otherwise, as global citizenship, we remain ignorant to the facts that govern our lives and control how we communicate and engage with others globally. Thus, the next chapter will convey the SWOT analysis of 43 countries' cybersecurity public policy. This research will enable you to gain clarity on the different approaches of governance being implemented around the world to safeguard citizen's usage of the Internet.

Discussion Questions

1. What inalienable right is encompassed within the liberties given to citizens in a democratic society?
2. Who developed the Online Privacy Law?
3. What does Directive 95/46/EC focus on?
4. What countries laws dictate the rights of citizen's freedom?
5. What is required for any country cybersecurity public policy to be effective?
6. Global laws governing the Internet and technology are?
7. When was the Electronic Communication Privacy Act enacted?
8. When was the Retention Data Law passed?
9. Who passed a law regarding Internet Censorship?

Case Study

With the effort deployed to research 43 countries' cybersecurity public policy, there are facts supporting the need to protect Internet users globally. Cybersecurity practitoners predict there will be 6 billion Internet active users by the year 2023, which is approximately 75 percent of the world population of about 8 billion. It is estimated there will be more than 7.5 billion active Internet users by 2030, which is approximately 90 percent of the world population. This calls for more protection to be deployed for these Internet users.

SCENARIO: A small state agency made extensive use of automated clearing house (ACH) transfers. The agency employees logged in with both the agency and user-specific ID and password. Four challenge questions were to be answered for transactions of over $5,000. The Manager was notified that ACH transfer of $20,000 was initiated by an unknown source. The bank was contacted and identified that in two weeks cybercriminals had made 15 transfers from the agency bank account. What possibly went wrong with the employees to capture the banking credentials? Based on what you have read in this chapter, what in your view is the most suitable public policy approach and why?

Notes

1 Online Privacy Law: European Union. (2020). United States Library of Congress. Retrieved from: https://www.loc.gov/law/help/online-privacy-law/2012/eu.php

2 Right to be Forgotten. (2019). Intersoft Consulting: GDPR. Retrieved from: https://www.gdpr-info.eu/issues/right-to-be-forgotten

3 Panko, R. R. & Panko, L. J. (2019). *Business Data Networks and Security* (11th Ed). Pearson Education, Inc., Hoboken, NJ, p. 4.

4 Whittaker, Z. & Osborne, C. (2020). ZdNet.com. Cybersecurity 101: Protect your Privacy from Hackers, Spies, and the Government. Retrieved from: https://www.zdnet.com/article/online-security-101-how-to-protect-your-privacy-from-hackers-spies-and-the-government

5 2019 Internet Crime Report Released. (2019). FBI.gov. Retrieved from: https://www.fbi.gov/news/stories/2019-Internet-crime-report-released-021120

6 Specopssoft.com. (2019). The European Countries Most at Risk of Cyber-Crime. Retrieved from: https://www.specopssoft.com/blog/european-countries-cyber-crime

4

43 COUNTRIES CYBERSECURITY PUBLIC POLICY SWOT ANALYSIS

Learning Objectives

- Comprehend the significance of cybersecurity public policy.
- Understand 43 countries cybersecurity public policy.
- Effectively assess the strengths, weaknesses, threats, and opportunities of 43 countries cybersecurity public policy.
- Gain clarity on the best methods to deter cyber-incidences with cybersecurity public policy.

In December 2020, global news reports conveyed that cyberattacks executed against public sector has increased. The latest victim was the United States Department of The Treasury. The attack executed enabled hackers to retrieve dozens of email accounts registered with the Department of The Treasury, and Russia is being blamed for this attack. Russia's current Cybercrime statistics report that Russia is a country where the government supports its citizens nefarious criminal acts, including monopolizing the Dark Web underworld for criminal espionage. These nefarious acts are enabling cybercrime actors to develop, deploy, and manage cybercrime syndicates, whose fortunes scale $500 billion annually. The impact of cybercrime is weighing heavy on how international laws and cybersecurity public policy play a role in how cybercrime is dealt with. When any nation state or country's government supports nefarious criminal acts of cybercriminals, that nation state or country's government bears investigating and scrutinizing. After all, many nation states and countries have already joined forces to develop, deploy, manage, and share cybersecurity laws and public policy that will enable all countries and nation states accessibility to a strategic cybersecurity public policy framework to adopt and model; to diminish cybercriminals' power and impact the risk management control and governance of cybercrime.

DOI: 10.1201/9781003259145-5

More than 43 countries have already begun the daunting task of drafting, redefining, editing, and revising national security cybersecurity public policy. Each cybersecurity public policy encompasses strategic plans that each country believes is the best methodology to assess cybersecurity vulnerabilities and threats, deployed against their country. While some countries believe strongly in the impact and power of cybersecurity public policy, many others do not agree, or even feel the need to develop such an approach to combat cybercrime, because the impact of cybercrime in that country remains low. With increased cyberattacks costing public sector over $100 million annually. More effort is needed to increase understanding the issues and concerns most invaluable to protecting and securing public sector information systems, information technology, artificial intelligence, virtual cloud environments, hardware, software, Internet of Things, 3D printing, quantum computing, WIFI, Broadband, geospatial, and Internet from victimization of cyberattacks.

One approach to understanding the impact cybersecurity public policy has on public sector control of cyberattacks is conducting a SWOT analysis on the publicly known and published national security cybersecurity public policy, countries shares with the public. Having access to this national security data exposes the strengths each country cybersecurity public policy has; points out the weaknesses easily identifiable; shines light on the opportunities embedded that bridges the gaps and provides clarity on the subject matters most important to governing cybersecurity risk management and cyberattacks, as well as exposes threats. Thus, this chapter assesses the cybersecurity public policy developed by Afghanistan, Australia, Bermuda, Canada, Chili, Croatia, Cyprus, Czech Republic, Dubai, Egypt, Estonia, European Union, Finland, Gambia, Germany, Greece, Hungary, Icelandic, Ireland, Italy, Japan, Kenya, Kosovo, Kuwait, Luxemburg, Malaysia, Nepal, Netherlands, New Zealand, Norway, Poland, Samoa, Singapore, Slovakia, South Africa, Switzerland, Thailand, Trinidad and Tobago, Uganda, United Arab Emeritus, United Kingdom, and Vietnam. Researching these public policies enables all governments, Parliaments, and Ministries to build upon the strengths within their cybersecurity public policy; strengthen any weaknesses, increase opportunities, and defuse threats.

Afghanistan

Population: 38,928,346 million (2020) * Worldometer - real time world statistics (worldometers.info)

National Security Public Policy: National Cyber Security Strategy of Afghanistan[1]

Year of Publication: 2014

Number of pages: 15

Strengths

- Having a willingness to adopt international laws & policy that increases the value of the current cybersecurity public policy.
- Being willing to build alliances with private sector to enhance the security strategies needed to effectively deploy risk management control.
- Complying with the CIA Triad (e.g., Confidentiality, Integrity, and Availability).
- Remaining current with today's trends in adopting cybersecurity policy, information security policy, and information systems policy.
- Deploying effective education and training programs to prepare future cybersecurity professonals and experts.

Weaknesses

- Avoiding every kind of unwanted or unwarranted influence from external government on cybersecurity task.
- Periodically conducting risk assessments & security standards compliance of the critical information infrastructure.
- Lack of cybersecurity laws that deter cyber-espionage.
- Lack of cybersecurity laws that deter cyberbullying.

- Lacks cybersecurity laws that deter cyberattacks.
- Lacks cybersecurity laws that control citizens from becoming cybercriminals.
- Lacks cybersecurity laws that deter cyber-terrorism.

Opportunities

- Building strong alliances with international governments.
- Enabling international education alliance that builds the knowledge of cybersecurity professionals.
- Bridging the gap of communication with law enforcement globally.
- Diminishing fear of citizen's usage of Internet for business, academic, and financial purposes.
- Increasing private sector trust in the government.
- Increasing revenue earnings for all businesses and financial institutions.
- Empowering the public sector with current cybersecurity knowledge, education, and training.

Threats

- Neglecting to stay current with international cybersecurity trends.
- Neglecting to update current cybersecurity public policy annually.
- Neglecting to pass laws and enforce laws that protect citizens from cybercrime.
- Limiting the education and training both private and public sector needs.
- Not updating information systems as globally advised.
- Neglecting to deploy strategies that are effective and efficient.
- Refusing to work with international governments on cybersecurity laws and policy.

The current national security cybersecurity public policy is limited in its approach to effectively secure the country from external cyber-attacks, cybercrimes, cyber-terrorism, and cyber-espionage. An effective approach would be to improve the current cybersecurity public policy and provide citizens the assurance; they seek from the government to feel safeguarded from victimization. In fact, Rob Johnson believes that making minor revisions has little significance. While major revisions significantly change the policy. Johnson also believes that it is essential to utilize the following information:

- **Exceptions and waivers**- evaluate the current policy for common problems relating to compliance. If standards cannot be met there is a problem with the standards or policy.
- **Requests from users and managers**: Obtain feedback from citizens who rely on cybersecurity public policy. This can include businesses, academics, and financial institutions Chief Information Officers, Chief Technology Officers, and IT managers who are knowledgeable of the standards and policies currently in place.

In modifying current cybersecurity public policy, Afghanistan can increase its cybersecurity strategies to align with international laws and policies that increase the security and risk management needed to successfully combat cybercrime.

Australia

Population: 25,625,028 (2020) * Worldometer - real time world statistics (worldometers.info)
Australia Cybersecurity Strategy 2020[2]
Year of Publication: 2020
Number of pages: 52

Strengths

- A willingness to invest billions to enhance cybersecurity in a ten-year timeline.
- Implementing improved methodologies to defeat cybercrime via the Dark Web.

- A willingness to increase government information systems security policy and methods of compliance and risk management.
- Developing and supporting the Joint Cyber Security Centre program.
- Providing information to educate the citizens about Internet of Things.
- Offering 24/7 Cyber Hotlines and Global Networking.
- Deploying efforts to defeat offshore criminals with International laws.
- Implementing the Cybersecurity National Workforce Growth program.
- Increasing rates of trust with local businesses and families.

Weaknesses

- Government information systems lack effective security architecture.
- State territories are lacking effective information security infrastructure.
- Health industry lacks increased information security infrastructure and policy.
- Too many citizens were victimized by cybercrime in 2019.
- There is an absence of cybersecurity policy for private sector to model.

Opportunities

- Enacting new legislation on cybersecurity and cybercrime.
- Enabling private sector to rebuild upon successful cyberattacks with government funding support.
- Increasing penalties for global cybercriminal acts committed offshore to deter cybercrime.
- Updating government networks to Cloud computing architecture to reduce security risk.

- Defining specific standardized technology-infused policy.
- Increasing penalties for businesses that govern, store, or share consumer's personal data ineffectively.

Threats

- Government information systems are not designed effectively to thwart cyberattacks.
- Decreasing re-verify unlocks potential threats to Australian's personal identities.
- The private sector lacks effective risk management control over Australia's personal data.

Maintaining effective information systems to develop, share, receive and store sensitive data is essential to managing a safe and secure information system. Staying current with trends in defining and deploying secure information systems will enable Australia's government to stay one step ahead of cybercriminals and cyber-terrorist. Updating the information system with increased software applications that utilize effective security models (e.g., Cloud computing architecture) is the best method to implement because this environment is scalable, cost-effective, and easy to manage. Relying on cloud service providers that deliver international services, backed with support, will enable increased assurance in the services delivered. Furthermore, educating and training essential workers to understand their role and responsibilities should be a main priority. Otherwise, there is room for human error to occur as a common practice. Thus, it is essential to collaborate with global universities and colleges offering current trend knowledge and hands-on practice developing, deploying, and managing cybersecurity public policy, information security policy, and Cloud systems security policy. As well as working closely with international governments to gain new concepts of education and training for increased information system security and development updating.

In fact, determining how policy is developed and implemented can help or hinder how useful the policy is to an organization. In general, policy is only enforceable if it is clearly designed, developed, and implemented. When workplace personnel are provided efficient training about their roles and responsibilities, the power is broader in managing potential risk and reducing threats. Quarterly updates and annual assessments should be common practice, and documenting all activities deployed to assess the information systems, can be instrumental in helping control cyberattacks. Working with the community and promoting cybersecurity awareness, education, and training will also help Australian citizens become prevention actors against cyberattacks and cybercrime.

With the establishment of the Joint Cybersecurity Centre Program there is an increase opportunity to build alliances with international cybersecurity programming. When all countries join together there is a renewed strength in numbers. Effective risk management control and implementation across all platforms utilized by government and private sector (e.g., Internet Service Providers, software developers, and e-commerce) will increase security defense and slowly defeat cybercrime.

Bermuda

Population: 61,994 * Worldometer - real time world statistics (worldometers.info)
Bermuda Cybersecurity Strategy[3]
Year of publication: 2018–2022
Number of pages: 42

Strengths

- Having the awareness that nation states engage in cyber-espionage for political and economic gain.
- Establishing the Cybersecurity Governance Board.
- Recognizing and adhering to industry standards.
- Enabling the public and private relationship to be a guide for developing and implementing cybersecurity and cybercrime legislation.

- Effectively securing the Critical Information Infrastructure within government and assuring these departments are adequately protected.
- Enacting the Information System Risk Management Programme policy.
- Having a strategic goal to enhance local and international cybersecurity collaboration and cooperation.
- Acknowledging cooperate and state-sponsored cyber-espionage.
- Creating the Cyber Tips program.
- Relying on a Monitoring & Evaluation Plan to monitor the progress and impact of the recommended objectives and milestones in the BC Strategy.

Weaknesses

- Relying on all stakeholders to enhance their individual capabilities for protecting ICT systems and data from current and emerging cyber-threats, could enable increased vulnerabilities in software applications and ICT systems to be exploited and impact both public and private information systems, cloud environments, IoT, artificial intelligence, and quantum computing.
- Lacking effective information sharing regarding system vulnerabilities, software vulnerabilities, audit vulnerabilities, and cybercrime incident reporting.
- Low-level amount of efficient and effective workforce training and education preparation encompassing cybersecurity, information systems security, information technology security, cloud environment security, artificial intelligence security, Internet of Things security, 3D printing security, quantum computing security, and robotic security.
- Conducting periodic reviews of all existing and relevant legislation, regulation, and policies and procedures relating to cybersecurity.

Opportunities

- Enhancing the exchange of incident reporting between public and private sector through increased communication i.e., forums, emails, phone calls, monthly meetings (e.g., Town Hall), etc.
- Extending the timeline to prosecute cybercrimes committed domestically and internationally.
- Enacting legislation that aligns with international jurisdiction to increase penalties, fines, and extradition of cybercriminals as a deterrence model.
- Enhancing workforce both public and private, knowledge, skills, training and education on cybercrime, cybersecurity, information system security, information security, cloud security, artificial intelligence security, Internet of Things security, quantum computing security, and 3D printing security.
- Adopting an overarching national cybersecurity strategy for the country by implementing standardized software usage for both public and private sector that enhances the ability to effectively decrease known vulnerabilities and exploitable systems.
- Utilizing all international laws and ICT framework and policy for monitoring cyber-threats as well as detecting and mitigating cyber-incidences, information security breaches, information systems security and breaches, cloud environment security and breaches, artificial intelligence security and breaches, and information technology security and breaches i.e., NIST, HIPAA, Sarbanes Oxley, ISO 270001/ISO 270002, GDPR, Homeland Security Act, and the Russia Federal Law on Personal Data.
- Enacting new laws that mirror international laws that enable the Bermuda government increased control to govern cybercrime, increase penalties rendered for violating Bermuda laws on cybercrime, as well as increasing fines for committing such crimes.

Threats

- Neglecting to hold telecommunication service providers accountable to global standards of data privacy and consumer information protection.
- Neglecting to increase education and training for elementary, high school, college, graduate school, and post graduate school learners.
- Failing to stay current with trends in cybercrimes committed globally.
- Neglecting to increase awareness of vulnerabilities enveloped within software and hardware relied upon in public and private sector.
- Neglecting to enhance knowledge of ICT systems, software, and hardware as years of innovation increase.

It is instrumental to manage the usage of all software and hardware with a due diligence to help decrease the impact potential cyberattacks may have on these systems and applications. Neglecting to do so can be costly and increase the cost for repairs and rebuilding systems and/or integrating new systems, because old systems were not effectively managed to deter successful attacks from being catastrophic. Working in alignment with global governments, Parliaments, and Ministries to align policy and laws encompassing software and hardware securities, system updates, and back-up practices and procedures, play a role in security capabilities and mitigation strategies. Without doing so there remains a system of vulnerabilities that will eventually become gateways to exploitable systems.

Thus, it is important to increase the knowledge and training of citizens who can become instrumental in governing these systems and securing these environments as needed to avoid victimization prior to being victimized. This requires working with the Department of Education or Ministry of Education to increase curriculum and instruction development that enables learners to gain the clarity and knowledge of subject matter. Doing so will enable an improved workforce that is prepared to defend the country from domestic and international cybercriminals.

Furthermore, it is essential to research world governments, Parliaments, and Ministries laws, regulatory, and policies encompassing all ICT, including cloud environments, information systems, information technology, artificial intelligence, quantum computing, 3D printing, Internet of Things, robotics, and geospatial systems, to remain current with trends in crimes committed utilizing these systems and to gain the ability to understand how these systems are being secured globally. As conveyed previously, there should be a reliance on authorized standardized software and hardware utilized throughout the country for both public and private system ICT usage, as a method of deploying increased security risk management. After all, when operating new software integration, if workforce utilizing such systems and applications are not effectively trained, there remains opportunity for human error to occur and create a victimization experience that could impact cost and budget spending to repair the system or infuse an entire new system.

Canada

Population: 37,907,438 (2020) * Worldometer - real time world statistics (worldometers.info)
National Cybersecurity Strategy[4]
Year of Publication: 2018
Number of pages: 40

Strengths

- Forecasting a 5-year cybersecurity improvement plan.
- Funding the Canadian Centre for cybersecurity.
- Establishing the National Cybercrime Coordination Unit.
- Rendering funding that fosters cybersecurity talent.
- Defending private sector systems.
- Working with the Canadian Cyber Incident Response Centre.

Weaknesses

- There is a low number of qualified cybersecurity professionals.
- Not having enough clearly conveyed cybersecurity laws and policies enacted.
- Canadian law enforcement lacks knowledge of current cyber-crime trends.

Opportunities

- Enacting cybersecurity laws regarding intellectual property.
- Increasing penalties for cybercrime committed offshore.
- Building alliances with international law enforcement and government to improve extradition.
- Enacting IoT laws and enhancing penalties for violations.
- Making quantum computing a national technology platform and offering training and education to private sector.
- Establishing a 24/7 Cybercrime Hot Line.

Threats

- Lacking efficient knowledge on quantum computing security methods.
- There is not enough zeal for cybersecurity industry talent pool to increase.
- Lack of quantum computing laws and policy.
- Lacking block chain technology laws and policy.
- Exposing security flaws of non-government businesses in the public policy.
- There is no national cybersecurity model to mirror for private sector.
- Lack of efficient funding to support public and private sector training in cybersecurity public policy.

Having clarity on a five-year cybersecurity improvement plan will enable the country to assess its weak points and strategically plan to reduce these vulnerabilities. This will also enable the country to improve its cyber-tactics to help manage the overall cybersecurity infrastructure. With the established framework created by the National Cybercrime Coordination Unit, there is an increased chance to collaborate with private sector to encourage more information sharing. This will be instrumental in helping decrease current limited data sharing.

It is just as important to increase the number of trained and knowledgeable cybersecurity personnel in both public and private sector. Building a strong team of professionals that understand what is needed to deter cyberattacks, cybercrime, cyberespionage, and cyberstalking, can be instrumental in building bridges internationally and reducing the number of successful attacks the country experiences. Building alliances with global cybersecurity firms, governments, and organizations that focus on cybersecurity and cybersecurity policy, is vital to securing the citizens of Canada and decreasing threats and vulnerabilities. This can also be instrumental in establishing a 24/7 Cybercrime Incident Reporting Hotline. This pipeline of data sharing will be a vital medium to help effectively manage data sharing.

Chili

Population: 19,196,553 (2020) * Worldometer - real time world statistics (worldometers.info)
National Cybersecurity Policy[5]
Year of Publication: 2017–2022
Number of pages: 29

Strengths

- Public feedback is integrated in helping to develop current cybersecurity public policy.
- Offering citizens free public WIFI.
- Promoting industrial and productive development in cybersecurity.
- Having an Interministerial Committee on cybersecurity.
- Maintaining updates on all legal and statutory regulations.
- Increasing offshore prosecution for cybercrimes.

Weaknesses

- Neglecting to update the cybersecurity policy annually with current trends in cybercrime.
- Current laws do not align with international laws regarding digital communication and technology.
- There is a lack of national cybersecurity professional organizations that collaborate with the Chili government.
- Lacking a 24/7 Cybercrime Incident reporting hotline.
- Lacking public policy regarding storage, usage, and sharing of Chili citizens' personal data.
- A lack of laws regarding the use of Security Socket Layers (SSL) on Web site Web pages for financial institutions and all service providers collecting and storing Chili citizens' personal data.

Opportunities

- Building stronger alliances with international law enforcement and governments.
- Establishing more public/private collaboration initiatives that educates and train everyone on current cybersecurity trends.
- Defining an effective model to investigate and prosecute cybercriminals nationally and internationally.

Threats

- There are not enough trained cybersecurity personnel within the country to help deter cybercrime and cyberattacks.
- Lacking an effective line of communication with international governments regarding cybersecurity, cybercrime, cyberterrorism, cyberespionage, and cyberstalking.
- There is a lack of effective public policy development on cybersecurity and cybercrime.
- There is not enough cybersecurity educational programming offered through universities and colleges.

Building stronger alliances internationally is a vital component to staying up to date with current trends in cybersecurity, cybercrime, cyberattacks, cyberterrorism, cyberespionage, and cyberstalking. Without a clear understanding of how to deter, decrease, and effectively manage cyberattacks, cybercrime, cyberespionage, cyberstalking, and cyberterrorism, there remains a clear path of vulnerabilities that enables attack agents to successfully achieve their attack methods. This is a costly impact on the safety of the citizens of Chili and Chili economy.

Taking the initiative to increase cybersecurity awareness across the country can be a dynamic approach to building citizens' knowledge of cybersecurity and possibly invoke many citizens to take interest in becoming cybersecurity analyst and specialist. Otherwise, there remains a need to fill open roles in the cybersecurity industry, which leaves the country vulnerable. It is just as important to define an effective method to investigate and prosecute cybercriminals, both nationally and internationally. Therefore, working with governments internationally is vital for the safety and security of Chili citizens.

Croatia

Population: 4,092,600 (2020) * Worldometer - real time world statistics (worldometers.info)
The National Cybersecurity Strategy of the Republic of Croatia[6]
Year of Publication: 2015
Number of pages: 31

Strength

- Increasing societies understanding of cybersecurity and how cybersecurity impacts public and private sector.
- Having a willingness to collaborate with all stakeholders (i.e., state authorities, legal entities) with public authority.
- Having a respect for the human rights of citizens in this new virtual dimension of society.
- Focusing primarily on public and private sectors.
- Possessing the strength of resilience, reliability, and adjustability.
- Having a clear application of basic principles.

- Having a clear application of proportionality.
- Taking the initiative to educate and train all Croatia citizens on cybersecurity.
- Having a strong act of critical infrastructure.

Weaknesses

- Inadequate periodic adaptation of the strategic framework.
- Having a limited government control over regulatory & laws regarding private sector cybersecurity policy framework.
- Lacking clarity on an effective approach to thwart cybercrime offshore and nationally.
- Placing the Ministry in charge over all cyber-defense strategies.
- Having limited number of national securities to manage cyberattacks nationally and offshore.

Opportunities

- Rendering funding to private sector to establish more cyber-security organizations to help educate and train Croatia citizens.
- Enacting laws and policy to hold Croatian Internet Exchange accountable.
- Enacting laws for information security management and citizen data protection in both public and private sector information systems.
- Building stronger alliances with international governments regarding cybersecurity and cybercrime control.

Threats

- Lacking a national electronic registration security policy.
- Having a limited number of trained and educated cybersecurity workforce in national security to help thwart cyberattacks, cyberterrorism, cybercrime, and cyberespionage.
- Government information systems need improved security risk management planning, development, implementation, and managing.
- Lacking multi-factor authentication log-in on all public information systems.
- Electronic financial service providers are not being held accountable under the Republic of Croatia cybersecurity public policy or any enacted cybersecurity laws.
- There is a lack of financial sector risk management infrastructure developed by the Republic of Croatia.
- There is a lack of cybercrime incident reporting.
- Utilizing systems of secret surveillance violates citizen's human rights to privacy.

Lacking an effective method of security and risk management enables attack agents to exploit the system and wreak havoc on the economy if the attacks are successful. Thus, it is important to build collaborative relationships with countries willing to partner with Croatia and begin adopting strategies that will enable effective risk management to become a vital component to secure the information systems of government and the private sector. Developing and enacting laws that require the private sector to align their security models with the Croatia government security models, can be instrumental in helping open a line of information sharing and decrease the fear of government.

It is just as important to assure that all government information systems are controlled effectively with security policy. This should include establishing access control and regulatory, as well as increasing multi-factor authentication access coding log-in to prevent unauthorized access to sensitive data. Establishing clearly written policy and enforcing private sector align with such policy, will also create an alliance of trust.

Utilizing the strengths deployed in all other countries cybersecurity public policy will build a stronger defense for Croatia. Otherwise, there will be a growing impact of cybercrime and cyberattacks that may cripple the economy and impact the ability to quickly regain control. Thus, increasing the number of trained citizens on cybersecurity is vital to positioning a workforce prepared to defend the country from cyberattacks and cybercrime.

Cyprus

Population: 1,216,942 * Worldometer - real time world statistics (worldometers.info)
Cybersecurity Strategy of the Republic of Cyprus[7]
Year of Publication: 2016
Number of pages: 15

Strength

- Recognizing the value of CIA Triad.
- Taking the initiative to build trust in Cyprus citizens, organizations, and businesses.
- Defining multiple levels of security across the country.
- Collaborating with the EU Council on all policy updates annually.
- Understanding the need of multilevel security defense.
- Consistently upgrading cybersecurity policy.
- Valuing the private sector role in managing cybersecurity across the country.
- Having a National Awareness Program for cybersecurity.

Weaknesses

- Neglecting to update the cybersecurity public policy annually in alignment with current cybersecurity trends.
- Stakeholders neglecting to stay current of facts encompassing cybercrime, cyberespionage, cyberterrorism, and

cyberstalking to effectively sustain an impenetrable cybersecurity defense.

- Lacking knowledge regarding a specific mix of threats that can arise in Cyprus.
- Neglecting to research cyberthreats globally and deploying effective security models to thwart such.
- Neglecting to define risk management models to secure threats and vulnerabilities prior to cyberattacks and cyberterrorism occurring.

Opportunities

- Building education and training programs and institutions for public and private sector to effectively maintain cybersecurity knowledge and information sharing.
- Assigning research institutions responsibility to help discover new laws, policies, cyber-incidence, and methods of combating those incidences.
- Providing the funding needed to effectively provide adequate on-going research and education in the field of information security and cybersecurity.
- Updating the National Security Cybersecurity Policy annually in alignment with international governments will help Cyprus remain current with information security and cybersecurity trends.
- Establishing a 24/7 cybersecurity hotline and incidence reporting system.

Threats

- Lack of usage of multifactor authentication on government information systems.
- Lack of effective cybercrime incident reporting.
- Ineffective research conducted globally on current trends in cybersecurity.

- Ineffective risk management strategies for both public and private sector.
- Neglecting to invest in educating and training citizens to increase the cybersecurity workforce.

Implementing an effective approach to cybersecurity awareness training across the country is a step towards effective risk management. Without effective risk management deployed across the country, there is room for human error that can open a clear path to vulnerabilities being exploited by external attack agents. Having a clearly written cybersecurity policy helps the country stay current with trends in cybersecurity and enables external governments to gain clarity on the methodologies being deployed by Cyprus government, to deter and control cybercrime, cyberattacks, cyberespionage, cyberstalking, and cyberterrorism.

Thus, it is important that Cyprus join forces with the EU Council and other countries to build alliances of trust and decrease concerns regarding cybercrimes being committed internally and externally. This also should invoke Cyprus government to take action to increase cybersecurity awareness with its citizens and encourage more citizens to become active in helping protect the country from external attack agents. A good risk management plan should include mirroring the actions of other governments to implement within the country's infrastructure. Doing so can be helpful for everyone involved and create an open line of communication.

Czech Republic

Population: 10.65 million (2019) * Worldometer - real time world statistics (worldometers.info)
Cybersecurity Strategy of the Czech Republic[8]
Year of publication: 2012–2015
Number of pages: 10

Strengths

- A willingness to collaborate internationally on cybersecurity and information security affairs.

- Taking the initiative to establish the Computer Emergency Response Team (CERT).
- Adopting international laws and policies that strengthen the cybersecurity and information security posture.
- Maintaining diplomacy.
- Respecting citizen's human rights.

Weaknesses

- Neglecting to hold both public and private sector accountable.
- 2011–2015 Czech Republic cybersecurity policy was not thoroughly developed to convey effective methodologies to thwart cyber-incidences.
- Lacking an effective cybercrime incident reporting system.

Opportunities

- Defining a cyber-threat early warning system.
- Developing and implementing a risk assessment & risk management system that is effective in thwarting cyber-incidences.
- Developing, deploying, and effectively mitigating national cyber-defense exercises.

Threats

- Neglecting to effectively train and educate citizens about cybersecurity and information security.
- Failing to advertise cybersecurity training programming nationally to invoke citizen interest in defending the nation's cyber-territories.
- Lacking effective cybersecurity policy strategies and planning methods.
- Neglecting to fund cybersecurity awareness training for colleges and universities.
- Neglecting to encourage citizens to take effective steps to decrease cybercrime.

Neglecting to encourage citizen engagement with cybersecurity is a hazard to the cyber-defense methodologies any country can possess. The limited data shared in the current cybersecurity public policy convey a system of vulnerabilities that can be easily exploited, if not effectively mitigated. Thus, it is essential to increase citizen's knowledge of cybersecurity and the importance of their active initiative to deter cybercrimes from becoming a national issue. While the current trends in cybercrime in the country are low; it can be perceived by external attack agents that the country is an easy target.

Increasing cybersecurity programming across the country is essential. Working with international law and policy makers to increase the depth of the current cybersecurity policy is also a valuable asset. While the country may be small in population, it is still a gateway for cybercriminals. Moreover, it is important to enhance the knowledge of those who are regulating cyber-defense within the country. Working with a knowledgeable team of subject matter experts who can help position the country against its adversaries, is invaluable to the longevity of freedom against attack agents.

Dubai

Population: 10,025,932 (2019) * Worldometer - real time world statistics (worldometers.info)
Dubai Cybersecurity Strategy[9]
Year of publication: 2017
Number of pages: 36

Strengths

- Illuminating confidence.
- Developing a society entrenched in cybersecurity risk.
- Having a willingness to work with private sector to win the war against cybercriminals.
- Effectively assessing the urban environment both natural and human cultivated assets, as well as the living experiences of Dubai citizens.
- Focusing on transparency within law enforcement.
- Defining a great vision of hierarchy.
- Establishing the Electronic Security Center.

Weaknesses

- There is an unclear understanding if cyberattacks primarily derive externally or internally within the current policy.
- Failing to build stronger alliances with international cybersecurity policy makers.
- Neglecting to embrace the international union of cybersecurity defense.
- Neglecting to educate and encourage citizens to play a stronger role in defending the country against cyber-incidences.

Opportunities

- Enhancing the value of Dubai's information security regulations, particularly for the private sector.
- Developing international communication efforts with countries law and policy makers on cybersecurity.
- Defining effective mitigation methods that decrease the current threat of cyber-incidences within the country.
- Funding cybersecurity awareness training for citizens to become more active in thwarting cyber-incidences domestically and internationally.
- Building lasting alliances with international law agencies to deter cybercrime.

Threats

- Neglecting to maintain current knowledge of cyber-incidences domestically and internationally.
- Failing to effectively educate citizens on their role and responsibilities to defend the country against cyber-incidences.
- Refusing to build stronger alliances internationally with law and policy makers regarding cybercrime.
- Failing to increase the penalties for cybercrime domestically and internationally.

The current approach shared in the Dubai cybersecurity policy convey effective strategies to thwart cyber-incidences, both internationally and domestically. There is also a clear understanding of the mitigation strategies being deployed within the country. Dubai shares a knowledgeable and well-prepared cybersecurity public policy that can be mirrored by international governments who lack this efficiency.

However, current trends in cyber-incidences continue evolving requiring increased methodologies to defend the nation against unauthorized cyberattack agents. Thus, it is imperative to continue increasing cyber-incidence knowledge and increase training for citizens. In doing so, Dubai can continue being the pioneer it is in combating and deterring cyber-incidences.

Working with international governments is essential for every country. Regardless of indifferences encompassing religious viewpoints. Cybercriminals do not have a genuine concern regarding religion. As a result, citizens are victimized and businesses and governments face increased economic catastrophe. Thus, it is recommended that funding continue being allotted to increase cybersecurity awareness training. Not just for citizens but for those responsible for protecting the country against cyber-incidences. Having a strong team of cybersecurity analysis and specialist will enable the country to maintain its position as a force to be reckoned with.

Egypt

Population: 104,454,842 (2021) * Worldometer - real time world statistics (worldometers.info)
National Cybersecurity Strategy[10]
Year of publication: 2012–2021
Number of pages: 9

Strengths

- Enforcing Article (31) of the Egyptian Constitution.
- Establishing the Egyptian Supreme Cybersecurity Council.
- Understanding that cyberattacks occur even if facilities are not directly connected to the Internet.
- Emphasizing the importance of working with "friendly countries".
- Having a willingness to train law enforcement about cybersecurity and cyber-incidence reporting.

Weaknesses

- Assuming only technological advanced countries possess advanced knowledge and unconventional expertise of strategic, tactical, and warfare preparedness.
- Not being aware of potential ferocious and sophisticated cyberattack methodologies.
- Neglecting to invest in developing an effective cyber-incidence reporting models that enables the country to thwart against cyberattacks.

Opportunities

- Enabling the Egyptian Supreme Cybersecurity Council to play a major role in assessing cyber-incidences within the country.
- Sharing all compiled research on cybersecurity publicly.
- Developing strong alliances with international governments on cybercrime and cyber-defense mitigation methodologies.
- Increasing the knowledge of citizen's ability to play a role in thwarting cybercrime.
- Improving how citizens access knowledge and training for cyber-defense.
- Working closely with universities and colleges internationally to enable citizen's access to reliable, trusted, and accredited knowledge regarding cybersecurity.

Threats

- Neglecting to stay current with cyber-incident trends.
- Failing to educate citizens.
- Refusing to work with governments internationally to develop stronger communication and information sharing on cyber-incidences.
- Failing to fund educational programs that enable citizens to become instrumental in helping protect the country against cyber-incidences.
- Failing to update the country's cybersecurity policy annually.

The current cybersecurity policy does not convey in-depth methodologies that prove the country can effectively thwart and deter cyber-incidences from impacting the economy and the democracy of citizens. Thus, it is important to deploy effective research to gain clarity on the methods being deployed internationally, to deter and prevent cyber-incidences. Doing so will increase the value of the current cybersecurity policy.

Working with allies will enable the country to improve its cyber-defense models and increase its ability to be prepared to defend the nation against cyberattack agents. This should invoke more time invested training citizens and encouraging more citizens to become active in helping protect the country. It is just as important to educate all current workforce on current trends in cybersecurity and information system security. While common cyber-incidences may be targeted towards individuals and businesses, the government has a responsibility to protect its citizens and their private sector entities from unwanted cyberattacks.

Again, investing in educational programs that increase knowledge of subject matter is important. Neglecting to do so can wreak havoc and become costly. Thus, it is important that the Egyptian government work closely with international universities and colleges who are offering effective cybersecurity training programs that can increase citizen's awareness training and their ability to play a significant role in defending the nation. Otherwise, there remains a clear gateway for Egypt to be a victim of endless cyber-incidence, both domestically and internationally.

Estonia

Population: 1,327,521 * Worldometer - real time world statistics (worldometers.info)
Estonia Cybersecurity Policy[11]
Year of publication: 2014–2018
Number of pages: 8

Strengths

- Having a willingness to cooperate closely and consistently with international governments.
- Developing a cybersecurity role model for private sector to mirror.

- Supporting the existence and purpose of NATO's Cooperative Cyber-defense Centre of Excellence.
- Enabling the Estonia Defense League with developing a cyber-defense capability.
- Mandating with government authority IT baseline security systems.
- Bridging the gap between public and private sector and enhancing crisis preparedness.
- Requiring service providers to conduct security audits to assure secure and safe Internet connections.

Weaknesses

- Limited clarity regarding how cyber-incidence reporting is compiled, assessed, modified, implemented, managed, and align with internal cybersecurity law and policy.
- Limited details regarding the prevention methods that will be deployed to effectively reduce security risks within government information systems.
- There is a limited strategy plan to authorize effective incidence investigation by law enforcement.
- There is a lack of mandatory legislation and regulatory statues regarding education and training encompassing standards in cybersecurity and cyber-incidence mitigation.
- There is a lack of a clear approach to effectively measure information security resources that are vital assets in transmitting sensitive data regarding Estonia citizens.
- Failing to enforce financial institutions deploy stronger security to secure the personal data of citizens financial records and banking information.
- There is a lack of enacted cybersecurity laws regarding all cyber-domains (e.g., air, land, sea, and space).

Opportunities

- Establishing research Think Tanks for cybersecurity incidence reporting internationally and domestically.
- Utilizing international research to effectively develop and implement strategic cybersecurity risk management plans, processes, and procedures for public and private sector.
- Require all private sector entities to align their cybersecurity policies with Estonia government cybersecurity policies and laws.
- Require increased cyber-incident reporting for private sector.
- Implementing a national Cybersecurity Awareness Day or month.
- Developing, implementing, and assessing annual public and private sector information systems policy that encompasses security measures.
- Implementing laws that require financial institutions to effectively implement security socket layer (SSL) protection on all financial banking institutions Web sites.

Threats

- Limited policy control over effective security of government information systems.
- Neglecting to enact laws that penalize offshore cybercriminals.
- Neglecting to enact laws governing information security violations on public and private sector systems.
- Avoiding international partnerships to share research regarding cyber-incidence and cybersecurity.
- Limiting the strength of Estonia cybersecurity policy.

The current eight-page Estonia Cybersecurity Policy does not encompass an effective domestic approach to protect the country and its information systems from cyber-incidence that can cripple the economy. Cybersecurity is impacting countries economic independence and requires an increase of information sharing. This is one effective method of improving the current cybersecurity policy.

Working with international governments is essential to deterring cybercrime and implementing laws that will invoke external cyberattack agents from considering exploiting the vulnerabilities, Estonia convey in its current cybersecurity policy. Otherwise, vulnerabilities will remain exploitable. Furthermore, it is essential to increase the education of citizens regarding cybersecurity. When citizens are knowledgeable of the role and responsibilities, they play in protecting the country, they take a more sincere interest in defending their personal and public information and entities.

European Commission

Population: 447,000,000 * Worldometer - real time world statistics (worldometers.info)
EU Security Union Strategy[12]
Year of Publication: 2020
Number of pages: 28

Strengths

- Having a willingness to work internationally to build global stability against cybercrime.
- Taking the initiative to make values and fundamental rights the basis of security policies.
- Acknowledging that security supersedes the EU boundaries and that to effectively secure such is vital to protecting the freedom and rights of EU citizens.
- Common Foreign & Security Policy.
- Common Secure & Defense Policy.
- Investing in citizen's equity and equality.
- Understanding that relying on traditional state actors alone will not ensure the EU's security.
- Cybersecurity Certification is held under the Cybersecurity Act.

Weaknesses

- Assuming that having a basic understanding of cybersecurity will help EU citizens protect themselves and their personal information and professional entities.
- Public & private sector reluctance to share relevant security breach and cyber-incidences with the EU government creates a national vulnerability.
- Lacking cybersecurity laws and policy that are industry specific (e.g., transportation, space, energy, finance, and health).

Opportunities

- Creating a cybersecurity system that is scalable, reliable, secure, and efficient.
- Improving legislation's approach to enacting laws & policy that commands adherence across all platforms of technology in public & private sector.
- Enabling the Commission to develop, implement, modify, and impose penalties for violating any new framework for both physical and digital information system infrastructure.
- Launching a satellite Internet WIFI for EU citizens.
- Enhancing cybersecurity laws & policy that hold Internet security providers accountable for the security of EU citizen's privacy.
- Improving education and awareness training of law enforcement regarding cyber-incidences (e.g., crime, attacks, terrorism, stalking, espionage, and warfare).
- Enhancing legislation to improve e-evidence usage, making it safe and secure from mishandling or tampering data during transmission and while at rest.
- Holding search engine corporations accountable for enabling the submission of child sexual abuse material.

- Increasing global awareness regarding the need to pass legislation to combat Internet sales & distribution of large quantities of bio chemicals, radiological, and nuclear material to individuals.
- Improving security for information systems that compile and store sensitive information.

Threats

- Lack of cyber-incidence awareness training and education in public and private sector work environments (e.g., business, health institutions, and academia).
- Lack of enacted laws holding technology service providers accountable.
- Lack of laws that increase penalties on cybercrimes committed offshore.
- Lack of technology standards for security infrastructure for public and private sector.

The European Commission is a leader in developing and implementing effective cybersecurity policy and laws throughout the world that other countries mirror. It is essential to remain vigilant in defining effective methods that deter cybercriminals from being successful in deploying nefarious acts that impact the EU's economy and diminish the democracy of EU citizens. The current trends in cybercrime are exploiting vulnerabilities encapsulated in current information systems. This is due to a decline in awareness training and education encompassing cyber-incidences and information systems.

Thus, it is essential that the EU Commission continue exploring effective methods to enhance knowledge regarding cyber-incidences and share these methods with the world. Establishing standards that others will mirror creates a union of reliance that enables other governments, Parliaments, and Ministries to emulate. Setting the path that all others can comply with enables effective information sharing and can play a strong role in how new legislation is passed for other governments, Parliaments, and Ministry territories.

Finland

Population: 5,545,191 * Worldometer - real time world statistics (worldometers.info)
Finland's Cyber Strategy[13]
Year of publication: 2019
Number of pages: 12

Strengths

- Having the awareness that cyberattacks can derive from state actors and not just external actors.
- Possessing the confidence to thwart cyber-threats in all situations.
- Developing the National Cybersecurity Development Program.
- Having a willingness to partner with international governments, Parliaments, and Ministries to help deter cyber-incidences.

Weaknesses

- Lacking a cybersecurity strategy for 2021 and beyond.
- Having a disbelief that cybersecurity is not meant to be a legal concept.
- Entrusting the Cybersecurity Director to oversee all architecture and deployment of a cybersecurity strategy to thwart cyber-incidence internally and externally.
- There is an absence of cybersecurity legislature for 2013–2021.
- There is a slow development and deployment of private and public sector cyber-incidence reporting system.
- There is an absence of legislation impacting the enactment of legislative acts and policy to deter cybercrime.
- There is no enhanced penalty for cybercrimes committed offshore or onshore against the country of Finland.

Opportunities

- Improving cybersecurity knowledge, awareness training, and education in all sectors and industries across the country.
- Requiring service and product manufacturers to provide consumers access to the digitized format of technology security instructions on products and services consumers utilize and rely on.
- Enhancing awareness training and education programs for high school and college students to increase the number of workforce personnel in cybersecurity, information systems security, and information technology.

Threats

- Neglecting to effectively train and educate citizens regarding current trends in cyber-incidence.
- Neglecting to collaborate with international governments, Parliaments, and Ministries on issues encompassing cyber-incidence.
- Failing to increase national cybersecurity awareness.
- Neglecting to stay current with trends in cyber-incidence deployed domestically and internationally.
- Refusing to encourage citizens to play a role and take responsibility to protect their information assets from unauthorized users.
- Failing to hold financial institutions accountable for the security of citizen's financial data.
- Neglecting to enhance penalties for cybercrimes committed offshore.
- Failing to support extradition of cybercriminals when cybercrimes are committed onshore.

Lacking an effective well-written cybersecurity strategy and policy is a vulnerability. This enables external attack agents to exploit information systems and financial institutions within Finland territory, without concern of retaliation or criminal prosecution. Thus, it is imperative to enact laws that will thwart and deter cybercriminals from launching criminal acts against the country and its citizens. Gaining clarity on the laws and policy developed, deployed, and utilized across the world is a gateway to understanding what others are doing to meet their demands and needs to thwart and deter cybercrime.

It is just as important to stay current with trends in cybercrime, domestically and internationally. Doing so will enable Finland's government to maintain control over the threats and vulnerabilities the country face. Having an effective strategy to safeguard citizens from victimization will increase citizen's trust in the Finland government. Encouraging private sector to play a role in sharing cyber-incidences will create a gateway of data sharing and provide an assurance that the government is doing what it can to help citizens remain victimization free.

Gambia

Population: 2,451,246 * Worldometer - real time world statistics (worldometers.info)
The Gambia National Cybersecurity Policy Strategies and Action Plan[14]
Year of publication: 2020–2021
Number of pages: 45

Strengths

- Having a willingness to adhere to the CIA Triad.
- Building a strong synergy between public & private sectors.
- Willingness to improve Internet connectivity.
- Conducting effective Situational Analysis Baseline Assessment.
- Rendering thorough consultation of relevant stakeholders.
- Establishing a national cybersecurity priorities landscape.
- Taking the initiative to draft a Cybercrime Bill in 2019.
- Establishing the Gambia Computer Security Incident Response Team.

Weaknesses

- A lack of effective awareness training & security culture within several sectors of government, conveys a lack of effective cybersecurity mindset.
- There is a limited enactment of laws on citizen's personal data protection online.
- There is no central cybersecurity reporting mechanism.
- There is a limited understanding of online personal information protection.
- There is no ICT security on critical information infrastructures.
- Neglecting to align cybersecurity & information system infrastructure with international standards (e.g., NIST, ISO/270001).
- There is a limited encryption/decryption infrastructure on government information systems.
- Neglecting to hold ISPs accountable for a lack of security management tools to protect end-users' access.

Opportunity

- Increasing education and training models that can be delivered to law enforcement regarding cybersecurity incidences.
- Establishing standardized framework on all cyber-domains to increase awareness and training models.
- Improving firewall host-based security configuration.
- Enacting laws & policy that require private sector to utilize encryption on all information systems and Web site Web pages (e.g., Security Socket Layers).
- Developing and funding research foundations, institutions, and organizations that focus on internal standards of cybersecurity components.
- Fostering international cybersecurity and information security relations that increase awareness training.

Threats

- Assuming Gambia can deter and /or prevent cyber-incidences without the support of international governments.
- Neglecting to enact effective cybersecurity & information security laws and policy that require transparency & accountability in private and public sectors.
- Neglecting to enhance penalties for cybercrimes and cyber-incidences committed offshore and nationally.
- Neglecting to fund education & awareness training initiative to build a stronger work force to help defend Gambia from external attack agents.
- Believing that deploying "periodic" vulnerability assessments will be effective.

Many countries are grappling to attain clarity on what are the best strategies to help deter cyber-incidences from occurring within their territory. While there is evidence that Gambia government is taking action to implement new policy to protect citizens from being victimized by cybercriminals. There is also evidence that Gambia neglects to increase cyber-awareness training and education to increase its work force and effectively prepare citizens to take an interest in helping protect the country from external attack agents.

Having a willingness to work with governments internationally will be a benefit for everyone. This is an effective way to increase knowledge of current trends in cyber-incidences and help prepare public sector workforce to build their knowledge on new methodologies to help the country deter cyber-incidences. Unless there is an alliance developed between other countries and Gambia, there remains a gap of communication that impedes on the opportunities Gambia can attain to effectively protect itself from cyber-incidences.

Furthermore, it is just as important to increase citizen's knowledge and awareness training. In doing so, Gambia can stay ahead of their adversaries and win the war on cybercrime. Thus, it is imperative to remain vigilant and have a desire to continue gaining clarity on cybercrime and cyber-incidences worldwide, to gain insight on what should be done to prepare the public workforce responsible for managing cybersecurity and information systems. Otherwise, there is an open gateway to increase cyber-incidences across the country.

Germany

Population: 83,924,420 * Worldometer - real time world statistics (worldometers.info)
Cyber Strategy for Germany[15]
Year of publication: (2011–2021)
Number of pages: 20

Strengths

- Being knowledgeable of the importance of industrial infrastructure capable of being targeted for IT and cyber-incidences.
- Understanding the need for international partnerships.
- Adhering to the CIA Triad.
- Stressing the importance of all players working as partners and fulfilling their tasks together.
- Establishing the National Cyber Response Center.
- Enforcing international rules of conduct, standards, and norms.
- Being knowledgeable that a mix of domestic and international policy measures will be appropriate for the dimension of deterring cyber-incidences.
- Having a willingness to work in concert with international law enforcement to deter and prevent cyberattacks and cyber-incidences.
- Willing to work closely with society to pool information.

Weaknesses

- There is a low-level value of protection on government information systems.
- Neglecting to increase financial service provider responsibility & accountability regarding public and private sector information systems, including Internet Service Providers.
- Neglecting to infuse security socket layers on all government Web site Web pages.
- Not allocating sufficient public administration investment for information technology, information systems, cybersecurity, information assurance, and information systems security.
- Neglecting to include academic in the ongoing growth and development of the National Cybersecurity Council.

Opportunities

- Investing more in education and training awareness programs that encompass cybersecurity, information security, information assurance, and information regarding all cyber-domains (e.g., land, sea, air, and space).
- Increasing law enforcement knowledge and expertise in cyber-crime and cyber-incidence domains (e.g., stalking, crime, attacks, terrorism, espionage, and child pornography).
- Successfully deploying the G8 framework to combat anti-botnet activities.
- Building stronger alliances with international governments to combat the growth of cyber-incidences worldwide.

Threats

- Lacking reliable information technology systems & components that consistently enable an ease of access to exploit vulnerabilities through unauthorized intrusion.
- Neglecting to increase research on cybersecurity domains (e.g., land, sea, air, and space).
- Failing to partner with the United States, EU, and the UN to pool resources on information systems standards, information security standards, cybersecurity standards, policy, and regulatory.
- Insufficient set of prevention methods available to respond to cyber-incidences across all cyber-domains.

Having clarity on the required security methodologies to safeguard Germany's government information systems infrastructure is invaluable. Neglecting to take the initiative to enforce compliance regulatory, which citizens will comply to, is not taking an effective approach to secure the country from external attack agents. The growing number of successful cyber-incidence being deployed globally continues impacting economies. Unless there is an effective strategy implemented to deter and possibly prevent external forces from targeting the country and exploiting its vulnerable information systems, there is room for catastrophic impact. Thus, it is important to define effective policy that convey strategic planning that aligns with global governments. When everyone is working in concert to manage the weaknesses engulfed within country's information systems, there is a decrease of impact from cyber-incidences.

Therefore, it is important to educate and train citizens, both public and private on their roles and responsibilities. Having resourceful channels that provide understanding of cyber-incidences, how to deter these incidences, and what methods should be relied upon consistently to manage these incidences, will increase awareness of current trends in cyber-incidences and hopefully encourage many citizens to take a more esoteric interest in aiding and protecting the country and its information systems, both public and private.

Greece

Population: 10,396,080 * Worldometer - real time world statistics (worldometers.info)
National Cybersecurity Strategy[16]
Year of publication: 2020
Number of pages: 15

Strength

- Defining and installing the National Cybersecurity Authority.
- Safeguarding fundamental rights and freedoms.
- Applying international law to Cybersecurity domain risk management.
- Engaging Greece in international Cybersecurity initiatives & actions for the enhancement of Greece national security.
- Having a willingness to effectively develop, implement, and manage international methodologies for cybersecurity practices.

Weaknesses

- Conveying in print that the National Cybersecurity Authority will revise & update the National Cybersecurity Strategy, if required, annually.

- Lacking effective cybersecurity domain awareness education and training for public and private sector.
- Revising the risk assessment every three years is a gateway to consistent vulnerabilities within the current information system and decreases detection of potential threats within those IS within that three-year timeframe.

Opportunities

- Enacting & aligning legislative laws and policy that encompasses cybersecurity for all cyber-domains (e.g., land, air, sea, and space).
- Modeling cyber-domain policy developed by the United States and its NIST SP publication series, as well as the ISO 270001, Sarbanes Oxley, and HIPAA.
- Outlining the strategies of the National Cybersecurity Plan with international strategic infrastructure.
- Defining national security policy for public and private sector to model and deploy within national industries.

Threats

- Neglecting to install security socket layers (SSL) on all government Web sites.
- Neglecting to enact legislative law, regulatory, and policy for financial institutions to protect citizens privacy and sensitive information with encryption.
- Failing to enforce laws, regulatory, and policy that require enhanced encryption on all electronic transmitted data exchange channels, including technology tools that store Greece citizens sensitive data.
- Neglecting to require Internet Service Providers enhanced privacy controls and security features on subscribers' technology tools.

> • Neglecting to require private sector stakeholders under law, regulatory, and policy to share cyber-incidence reports that encapsulate large sums of monetary damage & personal date files confiscation.

Protecting the rights and privacy of Greece citizens is a democratic requirement. Human rights are essential to a free society. Thus, deploying effective security methods, laws, regulatory, and policy are necessary to maintain these freedoms. When a government neglects to stay current with trends in cyber-incidences, it fails to effectively protect its citizens. Taking the initiative to educate and train, both public and private sector to be aware of cyber-incidences, enables citizens to effectively prepare to defend their technology, personal data, and deploy strategies that will enable the country to decrease the number of successful cyber-incidences.

However, when you neglect to update the National Cybersecurity Strategy, every three years, you increase opportunity for external attack agents to exploit the vulnerabilities within the country's information systems and technology tools. Furthermore, when private sector service providers provide technology tools to citizens that are not secure, it enables citizens to become victimized. And when there is a decrease in data sharing regarding successful attacks deployed against private sector entities, there remains a gap in communication that decreases the security of the country and its information systems. Thus, it is recommended that Greece willfully work with international governments to stay current with trends in cyber-incidences and align their National Cybersecurity Strategy with these governments' cybersecurity strategies. Doing so will enable Greece to safeguard its information systems and technology tools effectively and efficiently.

Hungary

Population: 9,647,307 * Worldometer - real time world statistics (worldometers.info)
National Cybersecurity Strategy of Hungary[17]

Year of publication: 2013
Number of pages: 6

Strengths

- Establishing the National Cybersecurity Coordination Council.
- Having interest in protecting national and international sovereignty.
- Having a willingness to take responsibility for cyberspace protection tasks.
- Understanding the need to secure cyberspace nationally and offshore.
- Acknowledging information warfare.
- Acknowledging the risk associated with cloud computing and mobile Internet.
- Relying on contingency planning and risk management.
- Clinging to international security methodologies to secure Hungary cyberspace.

Weaknesses

- Neglecting to define effective strategies to thwart cyberattacks & threats impacting cyber-domains (e.g., land, air, and sea).
- Neglecting to increase government control over public & private cyber-incidences through enacted laws, regulatory, and policy.
- Neglecting to align Hungary laws, regulatory, and policy with international laws that regulate security mechanisms to benefit Hungary's efforts to thwart cyberattacks across all cyber-domains (e.g., land, air, sea, and space).
- Neglecting to integrate private sector in the on-going Hungary cybersecurity efforts to defend framework for strategic deterrence planning, development, implementation, and management.

Opportunities

- Increasing awareness training across the nation that encompasses cybersecurity and all cyber-domains (e.g., land, air, sea, and space).
- Investing increased funding to support private sector organizations who can efficiently provide adequate education in the cyber-domains to build the cybersecurity subject matter expert pool.
- Enacting legislation to enhance parental control on all Web sites nationally to decrease child access to sensitive adult content.
- Bridging the gap between public & private sector to establish a secure collaboration of information security sharing, especially regarding information systems vulnerabilities and threats.

Threats

- Ineffectively enacting legislation securing government information systems.
- Failing to take lead to develop cyber policy, regulatory, and statues that hold public and private sector accountable for security risks.
- Not requiring financial institutions to effectively develop cybersecurity policy framework that secures Hungarians personal information.
- Ineffectively developing a National Cybersecurity Policy that conveys detailed steps and procedures to secure, educate, and train Hungarians, to securely utilize cyber-domains with caution.
- Avoiding the usage of international cyber laws and policy that can effectively help deter and prevent cyberattacks across all cyber-domains.

With a population of nine million+, it is important to take steps to effectively educate and train citizens to understand all cyber-domains. The current National Cybersecurity Strategy of Hungary is only six pages. This does not provide enough details on the strategic plans Hungary hopes to rely on to safeguard the country and its citizens from external attack agents. Having ineffective legislation that secures the nation's government information systems also does not demonstrate enough effort to secure the country from external attack agents. The impact of cyber-incidences occurring globally should be enough to invoke a more enhanced approach to secure the country from cyber-incidences.

Building citizens awareness about cybersecurity and cyber-incidences and the nefarious evils encapsulated with such, is crucial to gaining control over the power external forces can have. Thus, it is recommended to increase citizens knowledge of cyber-incidences through educational training to effectively prepare them to play a significant role in securing the country.

Iceland

Population: 342,420 (2021) * Worldometer - real time world statistics (worldometers.info)
Icelandic National Cybersecurity Strategy[18]
Year of publication: 2015–2018
Number of pages: 12

Strengths

- Implementing a "task force" to address strategies on cybersecurity.
- Having a willingness to collaborate with international authorities.
- Aligning strategies of security mechanisms with international information security models.
- Having interest in educating Icelandic citizens about cybersecurity domains (e.g., land, air, sea, and space).

Weaknesses

- Neglecting to enact legislative laws, regulatory, and policy that require standardized security infrastructure for public and private security that aligns with international laws encompassing cyber-incidences and cyber-domains.
- Neglecting to require Service License Agreements from private sector service providers to protect citizens privacy rights aligning with technology tools (e.g., software and hardware).
- Failing to require consultancies to meet Icelandic legislation on standardization encompassing data storage and transmission in alignment with international laws & standards.
- Neglecting to enact enhanced cybersecurity penalties for offshore cybercrime.
- Failing to set standards across telecommunication platforms for service providers to increase and improve network security, cybersecurity, and cyber-defense configurations for end-users.
- Neglecting to outline a systematic approach to enhance IT security for public administration.

Opportunities

- Establishing an Icelandic community cybersecurity forum for open dialogue of ideals, community resource sharing, and research.
- Defining a cybersecurity incidence awareness training and education program that enhances knowledge of international security models to deter current trends in cyber-incidences across all cyber-domains.
- Enacting legislation for each cyber-domain (e.g., land, air, sea, and space) that conveys detailed security methods and mechanisms to deter successful cyberattacks against vulnerabilities within the information systems of both public & private sectors.
- Enforcing collaborative relationships with public and private sector on all levels of cybersecurity management.

Threats

- Neglecting to effectively investigate all cyber-incidences deployed nationally and internationally to improve the information system securities for public and private sectors.
- Failing to enact legislative laws, regulatory, and policy encompassing personal data protection for Icelandic citizens.
- Failing to require financial institutions to increase data protection on all Icelandic citizens personal financial data.
- Failing to enact non-compliance penalties for Icelandic financial institutions to align with information security policy and law.
- Neglecting to enforce all software developed in Icelandic to encompass reliable design, particularly in the case of key elements of IT infrastructure.
- Failing to develop, implement, and manage cybersecurity policy on telecoms, utilities, and international aviation.
- Neglecting to model United States technology policy (e.g., NIST SP publications) to effectively improve cloud computing standards.
- Neglecting to effectively deploy legislation laws, regulatory, and policy that secures the Internet of Things.

While the impact of cyber-incidences may be low in Icelandic, there remains external threats that should not be ignored. This requires developing a clearly written cybersecurity policy that aligns with laws and regulatory implemented by the Icelandic government. It is just as important to effectively educate and train Icelandic citizens on their role and responsibilities in helping protect and defend the country from external forces that seek to exploit the vulnerabilities engulfed in current technology tools relied upon by both public and private sectors.

Ireland

Population: 4,967,302 * Worldometer - real time world statistics (worldometers.info)
National Cyber Strategy[19]
Year of publication: 2019–2021
Number of pages: 60

Strengths

- Acknowledging that flaws are designed in the operation of systems that lead to unexpected loss of services.
- Acknowledging the CIAA principals.
- Establishing the National Cybersecurity Center.
- Aligning with the EU Network and Information Security Directive.
- Combining security requirements and incident notification requirements.
- Broadening the Threat Sharing Group to engulf a wider scope of Critical National Infrastructure.
- Enforcing a standardization of information security, information systems security, and cybersecurity on all government information systems and networks.
- Increasing the education of Higher Learning students to increase the cybersecurity workforce pool.
- Attracting foreign direct investments.
- Respecting human rights as a guide for your cybersecurity commitment.

Weaknesses

- Neglecting to enact laws and policy that gives the government control over the public sector dissemination of software and computer system technology as a method of governing and deterring national cyber-incidences.
- Neglecting to define ICT (e.g., international cyber-terrorism) security laws & policy that encompass non-compliance penalties.
- Failing to deploy increased methods to reduce the growing cyber-incidences Ireland organizations and private sector citizens face daily.

Opportunities

- Enabling a secure policy plan to protect Ireland citizens while connected to and utilizing national broadband services.
- Updating the National Digital Strategy with current international laws & policy.
- Enacting legislation requiring financial institutions to comply with cybersecurity policy or face monetary penalties.
- Researching international cybersecurity law, regulatory, and policy and integrating components from international allies to improve and define an effective approach to cybersecurity and information systems security.
- Initiating an open-source system for reporting cyber-incidences (e.g., attacks, espionage, terrorism, bullying, stalking, and crimes).
- Rendering funding to establish organizations that primarily focus on categorizing and organizing industry related search engines to decrease the on-going dissemination of misinformation.
- Establishing an incentive to encourage more citizens to become subject matter experts and interested in working side-by-side with Ireland government and cybersecurity organizations, to build subject matter expert workforce that can effectively deter future technology infused attacks.

Threats

- Proposing effective initiatives to deter and prevent cyber-incidences and not effectively deploying such efforts.
- Neglecting to effectively require public and private sector to mandate "daily" written logs and reports of all activities developed, implemented, and managed to deter and prevent cyber-incidences.

- Not effectively implementing a strategy to regulate compliance with all laws, regulatory, and policy enacted to secure and deter cyber-incidences.
- Failing to introduce cyber-domain (e.g., land, air, sea, and space) policy and law.
- Implementing standards in cybersecurity and not implementing effective methods to assess the results and monitor those held accountable to manage architectures, infrastructures, databases, and information systems.

Implementing effective strategies to protect all information systems within the country should be a priority. Working in concert with global governments who share the responsibility of protecting citizens and their countries from victimization takes effort. Developing an effective workforce that understands their role and responsibilities will help increase the delegation of management and help decrease the continued successful exploitation of government information systems.

Italy

Population: 60,413,371 * Worldometer - real time world statistics (worldometers.info)
National Strategic Framework for Cyberspace Security[20]
Year of publication: 2013
Number of pages: 48

Strengths

- Acknowledging the requirements of involving private sector and its key role in sharing resolutions to current cyber-incidence trends.
- Acknowledging the fundamental characteristics of the cyber-threats and their asymmetric nature.

- Acknowledging the abilities, intelligence, and vicious attitude of a cybercriminal.
- Designating four district classifications of cyber-threats (e.g., cybercrime, cyber espionage, cyber-terrorism, and cyber warfare).
- Having clarity on the correct effect cybersecurity models embody to deter and prevent cyber-incidences from impacting cloud computing architecture.
- Understanding cyber network defense requires an effective approach to monitor risk management and assess accountabilities for all responsible of securing these environments.
- Identifying that some "States" are actively deploying cyber-incidences against other "States".

Weaknesses

- Lacking clarity on the four cyber-domains (e.g., land, air, sea, and space).
- Lacking current legislation that penalize cyber offenses offshore.
- Misinterpreting the authority government possesses to enact laws, policies, rules, and regulatory that govern cybersecurity and penalizes cyber offenses with increased penalties and fines.
- Ineffectively developing, implementing, assessing, and monitoring cybersecurity awareness education and training across public and private sector.
- Ineffectively penalizing non-compliance actors who violate legislation encompassing cybercrimes (e.g., hacking, sabotage, terrorism, espionage, stalking, and bullying).

Opportunities

- Enacting legislation that prohibits the use of cyber tools to conduct nefarious and criminal intentional acts.
- Enhancing legislation authority to increase current penalties and fines for public and private actors found guilty of violating laws, policy, regulatory, and statues relating to or engulfing cyber-incidences (e.g., cybercrime, cyberbullying, cyberstalking, cyberespionage, cyberterrorism, and cyberattacks).
- Increasing penalties for private sector that enables high security risks acts to occur involving personal data collection and storage.
- Developing clearly conveyed education and training awareness public policy for cybersecurity in the workplace for both public and private sector (e.g., NIST SP 800 series, HIPAA, Sarbanes Oxley, and ISO/270001).
- Promoting cyber-threats publicly across all media platforms.
- Creating a cyber-incidence report system that responds to and assesses, records, deploy attack defenses, mitigates, and manages cyber-incidences domestically and internationally.

Threats

- Failing to enact domestic legislation that penalizes cyber-incidences against government information systems, databases, and networks.
- Neglecting to deploy risk management control in public and private sector, and efficiently planning strategies to protect public and private sector when necessary.
- Under minding the authority Italy government has over assessing, planning, developing, and implementing deterrence methodologies against cyber offenses deployed domestically and internationally.
- Neglecting to audit all domestic agents utilizing and engaging in the reliance of data exchange.

- Neglecting to enforce encryption security on all financial institutions hosting sensitive data of Italy citizens.
- Failing to effectively audit the Cybersecurity Unit and all actors responsible for deploying standards in cyber-incidences.

To effectively manage cyber-incidences requires having clarity on current trends in cyber-incidences domestically and internationally. Working closely with international governments is essential to staying current with cybercrime trends deployed internationally. This requires aligning all policies and laws with international governments, Parliaments, and Ministries who are responsible for overseeing and enacting laws and policy on how cyber-incidences are managed. Neglecting to effectively train a workforce of citizens who are knowledgeable of cyber-incidences impacts the ability for Italy to thwart cyber-incidences and defend the country from offshore cyberattack agents.

Thus, increasing cybersecurity awareness training knowledge of information system security and understanding of all cyber-domains (e.g., land, air, sea, and space). Neglecting to protect the country from offshore attack agents via these domains leaves the nation vulnerable to endless gateways of access and can position attack agents to gain leverage over the databases, information systems, and networks hosting sensitive data of Italy citizens. It is important to install effective legislation that penalizes domestic and international cybercriminals who pose a threat to the safety of the citizens of Italy. Therefore, building stronger alliances with global governments, Parliaments, and Ministries, will be an effective approach to gaining control over the deployment of cyber-incidences targeted at the country.

Japan

Population: 126,265,236, (2021) * Worldometer - real time world statistics (worldometers.info)
The Cybersecurity Policy for Critical Infrastructure Protection (4th Ed) (tentative translation)[21]
Year of publication: 2017
Number of pages: 68

Strengths

- Outlining the context and plan of the current cybersecurity policy and its dimensions in the Table of Contents.
- Acknowledging that Japan's government should not expect private sector to rely on government involvement in operational strategies to defend the country against cyber-incidences.
- Having interest in strengthening international competitiveness publicly.
- Conveying a well-structured cyber policy in Table 1.
- The third policy composed of the five key policies.
- The ISACs organization and implementation encompassing information sharing and counter measures against cyber-incidences.
- Utilizing open-source publicized video sharing of cross-sectoral exercises as learning models.
- Establishing cybersecurity management guidelines that outline the basic approach to cybersecurity for corporate management.

Weaknesses

- Taking time to review the "main & measure sections" within the maintenance and promotion of the safety principles only once every three years.
- Relying merely on each CI operator incident response to maintain and enhance protective capability of CI based on knowledge learned only from experiences.
- Neglecting to effectively audit CI operators quarterly to assess their compliance instead of annually.
- Not enforcing the requirement of reports shared across industries regarding cyber incidences between public and private sector.

Opportunities

- Effectively implementing an information sharing system to bridge the gap between public & private entities.

- Building stronger trust with CI operators to decrease fears of retaliation for reporting cyber-incidences.
- Auditing CI operators responsible for managing the cyber-incidence reporting hotline.
- Developing increased cybersecurity policy education awareness training programs for public & private sector learning and comprehension improvement.
- Decreasing the lack of information system sharing by imposing a strategized planning process that can be easily improved as needed.
- Developing standardized risk management framework the private sector can mirror, such as NIST SP-800-37, NIST SP-800-53, NIST SP-800-39, and NIST SP 800-181.
- The Cabinet Secretariat maintains the deployment of continued analysis of spillover effects of CISs outages and assesses areas of improvement.
- Developing an audit reporting Web site where CI operators can submit reviews encompassing the scope of information sharing in & outside CI sectors.
- Utilizing all information sharing platforms to disseminate a wider scope marketing strategy to inform the country about cybersecurity policy and its impact on deterring cyber-incidences.
- Aligning current information system security policy with international information system security policies.

Threats

- Neglecting to effectively educate and train both public and private sector about cybersecurity, information systems security, and information security.
- Neglecting to effectively develop, implement, and manage risk management, as well as policy development, implementation, and compliance management.

- Failing to enact legislative laws aligning with international laws for cybersecurity, information systems security, and information security.
- Ineffectively auditing CIs who are responsible for overseeing the deployment of risk management control for information systems and cybersecurity.
- Failing to require all government Web sites to operate in alignment with international encryption recommendations for enhanced security measure.
- Failing to hold all financial institutions operating Web sites to conduct business or to provide financial services, to integrate encryption on all Web site Web pages.

The citizens of Japan rely on its government to protect their sensitive data from nefarious assaults deployed by international attack agents, as well as those living in the country. Neglecting to effectively safeguard this data is an irresponsible approach to assure citizens that Japan's government is aligning all security measures with the standards deployed globally by other governments, Parliments and Ministries. Thus, taking the initiative to increase awareness of encryption and the rewards for utilizing such will enable citizens to rest assure, they are being protected from unauthorized victimization. It is just as important to assure all government Web sites and information system databases are secure with encryption security application, on all data sources. This adds increased layers of protection that thwarts cybercriminals from gaining access to sensitive information that can be exchanged for Crypto-currency.

Again, it is recommended increased cybersecurity awareness education and training be standard throughout the country and programming be designed and relied upon to enhance the knowledge of citizens. Taking this precaution increases the security of the country and its information systems. Otherwise, there is an ease of access to sensitive data on both public & private information systems. Learning to rely on international laws, regulatory, and policy utilized by other countries, can be an improved model to enhance current cybersecurity policy within the country. Building stronger alliances and improving communication and information sharing globally, can increase trust and build stronger bonds between governments and their reliance on cybersecurity policy development, implementation, and management.

Kenya

Population: 54,409,874 * Worldometer - real time world statistics (worldometers.info)
National Cybersecurity Strategy[22]
Year of publication: 2014
Number of pages: 24

Strengths

- Acknowledging cybersecurity is Kenya's commitment to provide a safe and secure online experience for citizens who utilize mobile transactions to engage in foreign investing.
- Planning to deploy and operate a safe and secure e-Government system.
- Utilizing DigiCert SHAZ extended validation server for financial institutions Web sites to encrypt Web pages with a modern cipher suite.
- Acknowledging that insider threats are still a danger to Kenya.
- The National Cybersecurity Master Plan.
- Enacting Kenya's Information and Communications Act.
- Enacting the National Kenya Computer Incident Response Team Coordination Center.
- Establishing the National Certification Authority Framework.
- Acknowledging the immaturity of Kenya's government cyber posture.

Weaknesses

- Lacking clarity on international meaning of all cybercrime domains (e.g., stalking, bullying, espionage, terrorism, and hacktivism).

- Neglecting to enforce government of Kenya regulatory, laws, and policy requiring financial institutions to comply with data protection requirements (e.g., SSL).
- Neglecting to effectively audit public & private information systems security framework in alignment with international standards (e.g., ISO 270001, NIST SP 800 series, Sarbanes Oxley, and HIPAA).
- Ineffective cybersecurity emergency response methodologies.
- Conducting "periodic" cybersecurity risk assessments that should be conducted quarterly.
- Ineffectively holding service providers accountable for securing Kenya's citizens privacy protection.
- Ineffectively training government personnel on all cybersecurity standards, regulatory, laws, and policy framework.

Opportunities

- Improving cybersecurity policy training and education awareness for public & private sector.
- Developing a cyber-incidence reporting system for both public & private sector to contribute to.
- Designing effective consumer education and outreach programs that share vital information about cybersecurity and cyber-domains (e.g., land, air, sea, and space).
- Designing effective consumer education and outreach programs to increase awareness about cybercrime (e.g., stalking, bullying, terrorism, hacktivism, espionage, malicious attacking, and child sexual exploitation).
- Encouraging national leadership to become more involved in defining international cybersecurity visions, goals, and objectives.

Threats

- Ineffectively enacting laws that encompass harsh penalties for anyone found guilty of tampering, altering, or destroying undersea & terrestrial cable and network installations.
- Neglecting to modify and update the National Cybersecurity Master Plan with current trends and statistical research that improves resilience.
- Neglecting to partner with international higher education institutions to improve curriculum and instruction for effective cybersecurity programming and skills development.
- Failing to enact legislation that regulates information systems security, information security, and cybersecurity for all cyber-domains (e.g., land, air, sea, and space).

Utilizing modern cipher suite is beneficial towards increasing security layers. However, this should be deployed across all information systems, both public and private sector. It is also important to educate and train all workforce personnel on their role and responsibilities of protecting the information assets of the Kenya government, private and public businesses, academic institutions, and non-profit organizations. Establishing trust within the citizens of Kenya and enabling them to play a role in governing and protecting the country from adversaries who are utilizing technology as their primary tool to exploit the country's weaknesses and vulnerabilities, is essential. It is also essential to build alliances with international governments, Parliaments, and Ministries who, too, have a stake in the security of citizens and government information systems and information assets. Doing so builds stronger bridges and decreases distrust.

Focusing on the weaknesses and threats conveyed in this analysis, is a positive step towards redefining how to effectively secure Kenya from cyber-incidences. Otherwise, the country will remain vulnerable to victimization and endure increased economic setbacks that can be costly. Staying current with cyber-incidences and trends in cyber-crime is important to managing, your current National Cybersecurity Strategy.

Republic of Kosovo

Population: 8,718,064 (2020) * Worldometer - real time world statistics (worldometers.info)
National Cyber Security Strategy and Action Plan[23]
Year of publication: 2016–2019
Number of pages: 34

Strengths

- Establishing the Kosovo Association of Information and Communication Technology.
- Making international cooperation in cybersecurity a priority for Kosovo.
- Having the drive and passion to minimize and prevent cyber-threats in alignment with national and international partners.
- Sharing the basic meaning of specific terms compliant with European Union countries.
- Applying comparative methods and examining similarities and differences with Kosovo and other countries and member states.

Weaknesses

- Limiting Kosovo authority to impose enhanced cybersecurity law and policy violations with increased penalties, including monetary fines of $10,000 or more.
- Neglecting to enact legislation that deters cyber-incidences against government information systems.
- Neglecting to enact legislation that engulfs regulatory control of cybercrimes committed offshore and domestically.
- Neglecting to disseminate education and awareness training and marketing messages domestically that encourage citizens to study cybersecurity, information systems security, and support the country in its defense against cybercrime.

- Neglecting to require banking systems and financial institutions to infuse encryption systems on all information systems storing, sharing, and transmitting consumer sensitive data.
- Ineffectively educating Kosovo law enforcement about cyber-crime domains (e.g., stalking, bullying, terrorism, espionage, warfare, hacktivism, and child pornography exploitation).

Opportunities

- Enacting legislative law, regulatory, and policy regarding the protection of privacy and property of network users.
- Enacting legislative law, regulatory, and policy on information systems security for both public and private sector entities.
- Enabling the National Cyber Security Council to establish a strong international alliance in helping deter cyber-incidences.
- Partnering with international "friendly" awareness and education training providers in secondary, elementary, and higher education academia to increase domestic workforce personnel training.
- Supporting international Critical Information Infrastructure Protection.

Threats

- Regulatory authority of electronic and postal communication does not effectively audit the information systems procedures for receiving and recording cyber-incidences.
- Neglecting to rely on international standards for IT security and on critical infrastructure.
- Failing to reenforce confidence in Kosovo National Cyber-security Strategy and Action Plan.

- Failing to set accountability standards for information exchange and storage for Internet Service Providers (domestically).
- Failing to hold the financial, electricity, water, transportation, medical and health, and academic institutions accountable for the security of citizens personal data.
- There is a lack of effective assessment of cyber strategies.

Having regulatory, laws, and policy to instill governance, domestically and internationally, aligns with international governments, Parliaments, and Ministries. Staying current with these laws, regulatory, and policy will position The Republic of Kosovo to be a country that effectively manages its cyber-defenses against domestic and international cyberattack agents. Thus, it is important to increase penalties that will discourage domestic cyberattack agents from deploying actions against the country for nefarious purposes, as well as to decrease animosity that often rises among citizens against their country. This will also deter external international attack agents from targeting the country. Next, educating and training citizens on current trends in cyber-incidences and all cyber-domains (e.g., land, air, sea, and space). Establishing clarity with citizens is important. This enables citizens to develop interest in defending the country and creates a bridge of communication that is absent. Learning to rely on the defense practices deployed by international governments, Parliaments, and Ministries encompassing cyber-incidences, will be a key component to secure the country.

Kuwait

Population: 4,304,799 (2021) * Worldometer - real time world statistics (worldometers.info)
National Cyber Security Strategy for the State of Kuwait[24]
Year of Publication: 2017–2020
Number of pages: 39

Strengths

- Adopting every current trend in security as a precaution.
- Promoting the cooperation, coordination, and information exchange shared between international governments.
- Promoting a national cybersecurity infrastructure.
- Acknowledging the need for public & private sector collaboration to decrease cybersecurity risks.
- Integrating international practices of cybersecurity.
- Encouraging citizens to effectively take an active role in protecting themselves online.
- Increasing cybersecurity curriculum for universities and K-12.
- Maintaining risks assessments and conducting threat analysis for critical national infrastructure.
- Establishing a CERT team.
- Establishing the National Cybersecurity Center.
- Establishing a Security Operation Center.

Weaknesses

- Deploying a delayed response to the development & implementation of effective national cybersecurity policies.
- Delaying an enactment of legislation for cybercrime domains (e.g., stalking, bullying, espionage, terrorism, hacktivism, and warfare).
- Delaying development of national standards & criteria to classify information security technology.
- Ineffectively vetting all individuals appointed to the National Cybersecurity Committee and National Governance Committee.

Opportunities

- Developing stronger alliances with private sector and leading cybersecurity companies to stay current with cyber incident trends.

- Establishing a Cybercrime Incidence Reporting System.
- Enhancing improved accountability requirements for all Internet Service Providers to ensure the protection of data transmission across the Internet.
- Building stronger alliances with international governments, Parliaments, and Ministries on cybersecurity law and policy.

Threats

- There is a lack of legislative laws encompassing cybersecurity, information system security, and information security.
- There is a lack of enacted laws that enable prosecution of off-shore cybercrimes committed towards the State of Kuwait and private sector or individuals.
- There is a lack of shared responsibility for effective information sharing regarding cyber-incidences.

Lacking effective information sharing between public and private sector can impact the ability to efficiently plan strategies to deter and prevent successful attacks, despite the domain which the attack is deployed. When a country is prepared to defend its nation against external attack agents effectively, that country has a strategy that other countries can mirror. The United States and the European Union Commission has built a strong alliance of information sharing regarding cyber-incidences that enables these countries to continue increasing the knowledge of cyber-incidences as well as increase the volume of effective workplace personnel, who, too, understands the mission and goals of cyber-defense. Therefore, enabling citizens to acquire knowledge and awareness training is essential to the success of Kuwait's cyber-defense. Otherwise, there remains loopholes and vulnerable systems that can be exploited and successfully cripple these systems because of the low management of cyber-defense. Continued learning is the key to understand what strategies can be utilized to protect the country from external attack agents.

Luxembourg

Population: 631,686 (2021) * Worldometer - real time world statistics (worldometers.info)
National Cyber Strategy[25]
Year of publication: 2018–2020
Number of pages: 23

Strengths

- Establishing the Cybersecurity Competence Center.
- Ranking number 1 among 137 countries for innovative technology skills.
- Enhancing the security of information systems.
- Making cybersecurity an interministerial cyber prevention and establishing the cyber security coordination committee.
- Having a Cyber Diplomatic toolbox.
- Strengthening public confidence in the government and its strategies to defend the country.

Weaknesses

- Ineffectively auditing all cyber-incidence reporting administrative documents developed and stored.
- Ineffectively auditing State Intelligence Service administrative analysis and process information on cyber-threats.
- There is a lack of encryption mechanisms applied to government and private sector information systems.
- Neglecting to enforce personal data protection laws & policies for the financial and health and medical sectors.

Opportunities

- Defining "good practice guides", including behavioral, organizational, and technical measures in several languages.
- Enhancing cybersecurity and cybercrime domain knowledge across public and private sector.

- Enhancing cybersecurity and cybercrime domain education curriculum for colleges and universities.
- Effectively marketing cybersecurity and cybercrime incidence reporting nationally.
- Intensifying collaborative cyber-incidence information sharing efforts across industries (e.g., government, business, financial, health and medical, and academia).
- Enacting legislation of cybercrime laws.
- Increasing penalties for cybercrimes committed domestically and internationally.
- Performing analysis of specific risks based on the ISO 270001 in alignment with ISO 270002.

Threats

- Failing to require Internet Service Providers (ISP) to increase information security & cybersecurity methods and policy to ensure increased privacy and information sharing of consumers data.
- Neglecting to hold computer operating system manufacturers accountable for not aligning their security policies with Luxembourg government requirement benchmarks.
- Neglecting to provide incentives to encourage more interest from citizens to become cybersecurity, information system, and information security experts.
- Neglecting to partner with international governments, Parliaments, and Ministries to stay current with cyber-incidence reporting trends across all cyber-domains.

Internet Service Providers (ISPs) must be held accountable for the information storage of all Luxembourg citizens. Failing to hold ISPs accountable leaves room for these service providers to engage in nefarious activities cultivated by third-party partnerships that include exploitation of consumers and unauthorized information sharing. Enacting laws, regulatory, and policy that enforces compliance with the laws, regulatory, and policy developed and implemented by Luxembourg government, is a vital component to managing governance over the country and its information system databases. Furthermore, it is important to enact legislation that holds computer operating system manufacturers accountable under the laws, regulatory, and policy of the Luxembourg government. Neglecting to do so enables a gateway of nefarious acts that violate law and policy without concern for penalization. Thus, building stronger alliances with global governments, Parliments and Ministries and mirroring their efforts to deter and decrease cyber-incidences, will provide clarity on methods to effectively serve the needs of the country and its defense against international and domestic cyber-incidences.

Malaysia

Population: 32,598,981 (2021) * Worldometer - real time world statistics (worldometers.info)
National Cyber/Security Policy[26]
Year of publication: (n.d.)
Number of pages: 9

Strength

- Collaborative information sharing between public and private sector.
- Auditing Malaysia's cyber laws to address alignment with current international cybercrime trends.
- Effectively nurturing the growth of the cybersecurity industry in Malaysia.

Weaknesses

- Neglecting to enact laws that penalize cybercriminals for committing offenses under any cybercrime domain (e.g., terrorism, stalking, bullying, espionage, warfare, child pornography exploitation, and hacktivism).

- Deploying low effort to implement effective cybersecurity technology framework specifying cybersecurity, information systems, and information security risk management.
- Neglecting to enact accountability policy to help strengthen the monitoring and enforcement of standards.

Opportunities

- Sponsoring international cybersecurity conference.
- Enhancing knowledge for public and private sector encompassing cybersecurity, information systems security, and information security.
- Working closely with all international cyber incident reporting systems to remain current with global trends.
- Marketing cybersecurity, information systems security, and information security domestically via print, digital, webinars, billboards, and TV to increase citizens knowledge and interest in defending the country against external attack agents.
- Increasing domestic interest in cybersecurity, information system security, and information security workforce to build a stronger pool of subject matter experts.

Threats

- Neglecting to audit government information systems for effective security management in alignment with international government standards and guidelines.
- Failing to audit private sector regarding information systems security of personal data information storage and data exchange transmission.
- Failing to implement international laws and policy to enhance increased national cybersecurity.

Auditing government information systems that store and/or transmit public and private data is crucial to effectively secure all data at rest. Neglecting to do so enables domestic and international cybercriminals and hacktivist to gain access to these vulnerable systems and exploit them. This can impact the flow of information sharing catastrophically and cost tremendously. Thus, it is essential to deploy effective strategies that decrease risk and deter successful attacks. Implementing risk management is an effective step towards decreasing the vulnerabilities enveloped in current technology systems.

Furthermore, it is important to implement effective curriculum and instruction that prepares citizens to become cybersecurity, information system security, and information security subject matter experts. Working closely with universities and colleges to assure these learning institutions are staying current in industry related subject matter knowledge and trends, will enable the citizens of Malaysia to be instrumental in defending the country against international attack agents.

Last, it is important to align the current National Cyber Security Policy with international governments, Parliaments, and Ministries cyber laws, regulatory, and policy. Doing so will enable the country to stay current with cyber-incidences and strategies effectively deployed against external attack methods seeking to exploit the weaknesses within the country's information system databases.

Nepal

Population: 29,430,213 * Worldometer - real time world statistics (worldometers.info)
National Cybersecurity Policy[27]
Year of publication: 2016
Number of pages: 15

Strengths

- The ICT 2015 National Information and Communication Technology Policy.
- Understanding the need and value of risk assessment, risk management, and countermeasures to minimize risk and maximize benefits.
- Having knowledge of remote accessible cyber-incidences.

- Providing citizens updated information about cyber-threats and best practices to defend against them.
- Aligning all cybersecurity policy with international best practices.
- Implementing a National Computer Emergency Response Team.
- Building stronger public/private partnerships.
- Enforcing cybersecurity standards and guidelines to align with ISO 270001, ISO 270002, HIPAA, NIST SP 800 series publications, and GDPR.

Weaknesses

- Rendering control over the development of the National Cyber Policy to the Nepal Telecommunication Authority and not primarily the government of Nepal.
- Lack of skilled technology management experts in Nepal
- Deploying a slow progress to select, educate, and train new cybersecurity experts.
- Lack of offshore prosecution of cybercrimes and cyberattacks targeted at the Nepal government and Nepal private sector citizens.
- The Cybersecurity Working Group structure is limited to a low number of participants.
- Increasing the number of Nepal citizens who can be cybersecurity, information security, and information system security policy experts.
- Lacking information systems security policy that aligns with international guidelines and recommendations (i.e., NIST, Sarbanes Oxley, ISO, HIPAA).

Opportunities

- Increasing technology training programs (i.e., academia) that effectively prepares Nepal citizens to become instrumental in deterring and combating information systems vulnerabilities and threats.

- Enacting laws that enhance prosecution of cyber-incidences committed domestically and internationally.
- Building stronger alliances with international government and local authorities to bridge the gap of communication and the exchange of cybercrime incidence reporting.
- Aligning the NCSWG minimum requirements and qualifications for information security professionals who will serve as basis for the development of a related curriculum.
- Establishing a 24/7 Cybercrime Incidence Reporting System.

Threats

- NepCert neglects to stay current in cyber-incidences globally, which can reduce the ability to prepare for the potential attacks targeted at Nepal, both public/private networks, servers, and databases.
- Neglecting to develop an evaluation and certification program for cybersecurity services, products, and systems that can be updated as needed and remain relevant to current trends in technology usage, crime, and attack methodologies.
- Not taking the authority to increase penalties for cybercrimes committed domestically and internationally.
- Neglecting to educate primary and high school students annually about cybersecurity is not an effective approach to preparing high school students to understand how to effectively deter and prevent cybersecurity breaches or how to combat vulnerabilities engulfed in the technology, they rely on.
- Neglecting to educate Nepal private citizens on the increased need to configure all Web browsers for additional layers of security that helps reduce cyber-incidences.
- Failing to develop accountability policy for Internet Service Providers who control the Internet access of end-users.

Implementing effective methods to educate and train Nepal citizens is crucial to overcoming the increased cyber-incidences the country faces. When the country has increased its workforce and effectively prepared the workforce to manage their role and responsibilities in alignment with government laws, regulatory, and policy. It becomes easier to effectively manage and protect both public and private sector from victimization. This also helps decrease successful cyber-incidences, which can lower the risks and vulnerabilities encompassed with, public and private sector, information systems, networks, and databases.

With the increased transition to cloud computing systems, Nepal should also increase education and training awareness on this subject, to prepare citizens to understand this environment and the security requirements for this service, infrastructure, and platforms. Having a risk management plan that encompasses all components of cybersecurity, information systems, information systems security, information technology, and cloud computing architecture, enables Nepal to stay current with trends in cyber-incidences and decrease budget spending on the preparation and continued efforts to deter the country from being targeted by external cyberattack agents.

Netherlands

Population 17,157,038 * Worldometer - real time world statistics (worldometers.info)
An Integrated International Security Strategy[28]
Year of publication: 2018–2022
Number of pages: 22

Strengths

- Defining the Integrated International Security Strategy.
- Establishing prevention, defense, and strength as strategic pillars.
- Acknowledging that threats to the Netherlands and the Kingdom are almost always related to developments in the international arena.
- Acknowledging that religion-inspired terrorism is a major threat.
- Cyber Diplomacy.

Weaknesses

- Submitting only a 2-year report regarding the IISS to the House of Representatives.
- The Scientific Council of Government Policy confesses publicly that the security situation in the Netherlands has deteriorated, exposing this weakness to international cybercriminals.

Opportunities

- Utilizing the high-grade knowledge the Netherlands embodies to increase resilience, cybersecurity awareness training, and invoke interest in building citizens desire to become cybersecurity subject matter experts.
- Increasing laws that encapsulate concerns about the Internet of Things (IoT), smart grids, robotics, and increasing penalties for cybercriminals who violate laws domestically and internationally.
- Implementing a strategic plan and framework to effectively integrate 3D (defense, diplomacy, and development) into international cybersecurity strategies planning and deterrence methodologies.

Threats

- The rise of hybrid conflicts and tension within the Netherlands and Europe are increasingly impacting national security.
- Substantial level of terrorist attacks (i.e., hostile foreign intervention).
- Dependency on multilateral systems that do not and have not implemented effective national security and cybersecurity public policy.
- The increase of a multipolar order is impacting multilateral action.

- Lacking understanding of international relations and the consequences for the international legal order of national security and cybersecurity.
- Mass population of technically non-proficient and computer literate citizens.
- Having a lack of effective partnering in public/private sector on cybersecurity public policy development, implementation, and management.
- There is an increase in political and economic espionage and cybercrime.
- There is an increase in digital political espionage.
- There is an increase in military technology utilized to exploit domestic and foreign territory.

The best approach to secure the Netherlands and its public and private sector information systems, networks, and databases, is staying current with cyber-defense trends being developed, implemented, and managed globally. The increase of cybercrimes invokes a need to remain diligent in understanding the methods of attack being deployed globally. This requires having a workforce that is aware of cyber-incidences and that understand the value of keeping policy, law, and regulatory current with efforts of risk management deployed by NATO, EU, and the UN. Neglecting to do so can be costly.

An effective approach is developing, implementing, and managing the current Integrated International Security Strategy. However, this too, must be updated annually and convey in-depth clarity on all relevant issues impacting the country and its national security, including cybersecurity and information systems security. With the continued reliance on cloud computing SaaS, PaaS, and IaaS, there is a need to continue educating and training workforce personnel on the role and responsibilities, they have in defending the country from external cyberattack agents. Therefore, building alliances with global governments is essential. Not only will this enable the country to stay current with trends in cyber-incidences. It will enable an increase of communication regarding crimes and methods of cyberattack. Information sharing is vital to helping educate and train all countries to effectively continue defending their territories, information systems, networks, databases, artificial intelligence, cloud computing architecture, Internet of Things, hardware, software, and information technology.

New Zealand

Population: 4,868,653 * Worldometer - real time world statistics (worldometers.info)
New Zealand's Cyber Security Strategy 2019[29]
Year of publication: 2019
Number of pages: 17

Strengths

- Acknowledging that "good cybersecurity is essential".
- Acknowledging that cybersecurity is not simply an IT issue.
- Defining a cybersecurity policy that encompasses value & clarity on the role cybersecurity policy has on governance in New Zealand.
- Acknowledging Artificial Intelligence (AI) as a vital component to cybersecurity.
- Acknowledging quantum computing requires increased security.
- Understanding the risks associated with Artificial Intelligence (AI), quantum computing, and Internet of Things (IOT).
- Understanding that state actors are making the most of cyber-enabled tools to steal information, spread disinformation, and deploy attacks.
- Incorporating case study within the current New Zealand Cyber Security Strategy.
- Being aware that government is instrumental in managing cyberattacks.
- Acknowledging the need to collaborate with the private sector to minimize harm & disruption.
- Being aware that financial losses, reputational damage, loss of intellectual property, and disruption to critical services is crucial components that need effective mitigation strategies.
- Being knowledgeable of malware attacks globally and staying current with trends in malware attack models.

- Establishing the National Cyber Security Centre.
- Establishing the National Cyber Policy Office.
- Establishing the CERT NZ.
- Establishing the Government Community Security Bureau's deployment of CORTEX services.
- Establishing Malware-Free Networks.
- Increasing cybercrime tracing for New Zealand police.
- Helping small business learn about cybersecurity.
- Being aware that social engineering is a gateway to enable cyber criminals.
- Working closely with citizens to increase cybersecurity awareness.
- Respecting human rights.
- Respecting people's privacy.
- Honoring Internet law.

Weaknesses

- Minimum focus on information systems management.
- Minimum focus on information security.
- Zero focus on cloud security.
- Zero focus on "all" cyber-domains i.e., space, land, sea, air.
- Zero focus on policy & law that governs all cyber-domains.
- Zero focus on enacting law & policy to increase penalties for cybercriminals who target domestically & internationally.
- Zero focus on open share of extradition for cybercriminals internationally.

Opportunities

- Increasing laws & policy that protect public & private sector information systems.
- Increasing laws & policy that protect public & private sector cloud SaaS, PaaS, and IaaS.

- Rendering increased funding, grants, and scholarships for academic institutions and organizations to increase workforce preparation and training for cybersecurity, information system management, information security, Artificial Intelligence (AI), quantum computing, and cloud SaaS, PaaS, IaaS security.
- Increasing penalties for international cybercriminals.
- Increasing ease of extradition for cybercriminals.

Threats

- The lack of laws, regulatory, and policy that holds attack agents accountable for deploying attacks on public and private information systems, cloud SaaS, PaaS, and IaaS, Internet of Things (IOT), and Artificial Intelligence (AI), leaves a gateway for exploitation without fear of repercussion.
- There is a lack of focus on education and training on the subject matters conveyed above, which are essential security components of any cybersecurity strategy.
- Lack of focus on requiring financial institutions to implement effective encryption on all electronic information systems, provides an ease of exploitation of such, both domestically and internationally.
- Lack of annual auditing on financial institutions provides an ease of access for exploitation.
- Lack of annual audit of public & private sector information systems, cloud infrastructure, Artificial Intelligence (AI), and Internet of Things (IOT).

Effective security methodologies deployed across all information systems is a requirement that cannot be ignored. In the current climate of cybercrime and cyber-terrorism, cybercriminals are gaining knowledge on methods of attack from the free exchange of data sharing over the Internet. When information systems are not kept secure with the current trends and methods deployed internationally, this enables access to sensitive data sources that can be exploited and cost tremendously in repair, if possible. The old approach to security methods are not as effective when software is being developed to enable cybercriminals ease of access to data sources.

Additionally, there is a tremendous degree of strengths enveloped in this current Cyber Security Strategy that can help decrease the current weaknesses. However, the threats are important enough to focus more attention on and make increased modifications that will increase the security of these technology tools and systems. Thus, it is recommended that more attention is directed towards building stronger alliances with international governments and the public sector who manufactures these software applications, to acquire clarity on how to effectively mitigate these threats and increase protective methods of security within the country and externally. In doing so, New Zealand will continue being a low-level impenetrability system.

Norway

Population: 5,471,458 * Worldometer - real time world statistics (worldometers.info)
National Cyber Security Strategy for Norway[30]
Year of publication: 2003–2017
Number of pages: 21

Strengths

- Being the first country to enact a cybersecurity strategy.
- Effectively deploying updates to the National Cyber Security Strategy.
- Enforcing public/private, civilian-military, and international cooperation.
- Effectively educating private sector on how to utilize technology safely & securely.
- Being aware that robotization, sensor technology, 3D printing, and Artificial Intelligence (AI) requires significant focus & understanding to effectively secure these technology tools.
- Acknowledging cloud solutions.
- Acknowledging third party outsourcing in other countries.

- Publishing the annual Norwegian National Security Authority-Comprehensive Cybersecurity Risk Assessment.
- Knowing that threat agents are also state actors.
- Acknowledging the need for strong international collaboration.
- Establishing the Joint Cyber Coordination Centre.
- Enforcing everyone to take an active role in securing their information and personal data.
- Encouraging increased collaboration between military and civilian society.
- Recommending exchange of cyber-incidence data sharing and awareness training.
- Having a willfulness to work with international governments to deter and penalize cybercriminals.

Weaknesses

- The Annual Comprehensive Cybersecurity Risk Assessment does not encompass current trends in international cyber-crime incidences.
- Cyberattacks on civilian infrastructure may pose a challenge to Norway's national security.
- Neglecting to hold public sector accountable for citizens privacy protection and sensitive data collecting.

Opportunities

- Increasing cyber incident data sharing with private sector.
- Staying current with domestic & international cybersecurity trends.
- Increasing knowledge of information systems security, information systems management, and cloud SaaS, PaaS, and IaaS.
- Integrating international laws & policy that govern cloud security (i.e., NIST SP 800 series).

- Requiring public service providers to report and/or share audit reports with authorities to assure increased knowledge of deployed strategies that effectively manage the security of these systems.

Threats

- There is no focus rendered towards information systems or cloud security.
- There is no focus on increasing penalties for cybercriminals internationally who target Norway.
- There is no focus on increasing knowledge of deterring cyber-incidences within all cyber-domains (i.e., land, air, sea, and space).

The current cybersecurity strategy is well conveyed and provides clarity on the important components considered in protecting and deterring cyber-incidences within Norway. This is proven in the minimized number of weaknesses and threats. However, focus must be given to increasing education and training of new workforce personnel who can be instrumental in helping Norway, public and private sector, effectively deter and mitigate successful cyber-incidences, no matter where those incidences occur. With the four primary domains of cybersecurity being land, air, sea, and space, each one of these domains require effective law, regulatory, and policy to effectively govern the safety and security of Norway's technology tools and systems.

There is also a low-level of cybercrime impacting the economy of the country. Increasing citizens knowledge of the subject matter will enable them to play a role in defending the country from external attack agents. This should include increasing knowledge of international methods of security defense encompassing all technology tools and systems relied upon to conduct daily public and private service and business operations.

One effective model that should play a pivotal role in protecting the country, is staying current with trends of cybercrimes and cyber-terrorist act being deployed worldwide. This requires having access to NATO, EU, and the UN laws, regulatory, and policy. It is just as important to stay current with trends in software manufacturers applications. Having knowledge on how these applications can be monopolized to enable cybercriminals to deploy successful attacks is crucial. Furthermore, it is imperative that Internet Service Providers (ISP) delivering Internet and broadband services within the country, have a clearly conveyed Service Level Agreement developed and shared with both public and private sector, to decrease concerns of antitrust and assure alignment with Norway's laws, regulatory, and policy. Thus, managing an alliance with international governments is vital to staying ahead of cybercriminals. Most importantly, deploying effective audit efforts will help Norway remain vigil in defending its information systems, cloud SaaS, IaaS, and PaaS, Artificial Intelligence (AI), Internet of Things (IOT), networks, databases, hardware, software, and information technology.

Poland

Population: 37,798,313 * Worldometer - real time world statistics (worldometers.info)
Cybersecurity Strategy of the Republic of Poland[31]
Year of publication: 2019–2024
Number of pages: 31

Strengths

- Establishing the National Cybersecurity System.
- Focusing on mobile networks.
- Acknowledging the value of data sharing internationally.
- Acknowledging the value of information systems.
- Acknowledging that cybercrime is being committed by government institutions and armed forces.
- Adopting the policy for the Protection of Cyberspace of the Republic of Poland.
- Adopting the National Framework of Cybersecurity Policy for the Republic of Poland for 2017–2022.
- Guaranteeing citizens right to privacy.
- Enhancing and developing the National Cybersecurity System.

- Building confidence with private sector in the government.
- Focusing on protecting information as a vital asset to the Republic of Poland.
- Building public awareness in Cybersecurity.
- Holding digital service providers accountable.
- Establishing the National Critical Infrastructure Protection program.
- Rendering the Government Plenipotentiary of Cybersecurity to verify efficiency of functioning national security systems.

Weaknesses

- National cybersecurity standards and technical requirements do not encompass Artificial Intelligence (AI), 3D printing, machine learning, quantum computing, cloud computing, or Internet of Things (IOT).
- There is a lack of law, regulatory, and policy that governs all cyber-domains (i.e., land, air, sea, and space).
- Conducting periodic audits are not as effective as quarterly or annually for both public/private sectors.
- Conducting periodic test is not enough to assure all information systems, software, hardware, mobile and telecommunication systems are efficiently secure.

Opportunities

- Increasing globalized support of development, implementation, and management of cybersecurity, information systems, information security, and cloud computing education programs for K-12, colleges and universities, and post graduate programming can increase information education and training attainment that impacts how effective all efforts are received and deployed.

- Being a pioneer in the on-going development of communication and data sharing of international deterrence and defense against globalized cyber-incidences.
- Increasing cyber-domain policy that governs all cyber-domains (i.e., land, air, sea, and space).
- Establishing a month for cybersecurity awareness that encompasses information security, information systems, cloud computing, Artificial Intelligence (AI), Internet of Things (IOT), and quantum computing.

Threats

- There is a lack of focus on adopting policy and law governing the protection of sensitive data for medical records (i.e., HIPAA).
- There is a low-level of focus follow-up of audits and effective management of assessments of current risk management strategies and mitigation methodologies.
- Neglecting to integrate Security Socket Layers (SSL) and additional encryption models on all public/private information systems, IOT, AI, and cloud SaaS, PaaS, and IaaS.

Current models relied upon to secure the country from external attack agents continues to play a role in how effective deterrence methods defeat the cyberattackers. Due to the lack of adoption of law and policy to protect sensitive data of medical files, there is a gateway of access to data that can be exploited globally. Thus, enhancing protection of this environment should be essential. It is just as important to focus more attention on implementing effective audit methods. NATO, EU, and the UN share open-source auditing practices that should become useful in helping establish new methods of information asset protection of all sensitive information databases. Quite often when countries lack effective trained and educated workforce personnel, these environments become neglected and havens for misuse. Thus, it is essential to increase security awareness training for these data source files as well as increase knowledge building that increases citizens awareness of the value of securing data at rest.

It is just as invaluable to increase financial institutions requirements for Security Socket Layers (SSL) on all Web site Web pages, to decrease the ability for cybercriminals to gain access to these environments and exploit them. Financial institutions may be private environments but due to the degree of sensitive data that is stored on those information systems, it is vital that government takes an increased effort to align laws and policy that impact how these institutions manage financial data and transactions.

New trends in software development can be a daunting task to understand. Thus, it is important that Poland manages strong relationships with software developers and manufacturing corporations to remain vigilant in understanding what steps must be taken to effectively secure these technology tools and systems. If possible, the Poland government should begin developing its own software applications to increase security on all information systems and cloud SaaS, PaaS, and IaaS. Doing so will enhance the ability of Poland to increase its security methods and decrease its vulnerabilities.

Rwanda

Population: 13,325,584 * Worldometer - real time world statistics (worldometers.info)
Information Communication Technology Sector Strategic Plan[32]
Year of publication: 2018–2024
Number of pages: 51

Strengths

- Establishing Rwanda as a globally competitive knowledge-based economy.
- Strengthening capacity, service delivery, and accountability of public institutions.
- Increasing penetration testing to 39.76% mid 2017 up from 7% in 2011.
- Improving e-Government accessibility.
- Using ICT pillars as structure to achieve optimal goals.
- Harmonizing ICT legislation across the region.

Weaknesses

- Mobil subscriptions increased at 9.7 million from 2010–2017 while there was a lack of service provider accountability and security policy alignment with the government of Rwanda cybersecurity law and policy.
- There is a lack of audit filter optic managing private sector enterprises to assess encryption and security methods and assure these tools are being deployed effectively and efficiently.
- Increasing broadband usage across Rwanda requires increased law and policy to secure privacy for all citizens and to assure citizens human rights are not violated.
- Neglecting to increase auditing of broadband service providers to assure they are operating in compliance with law and policy both domestically and internationally.
- The low-level digital citizens literacy imposes a national security risk and enables increased vulnerabilities across all technology tools and systems relied upon in Rwanda.
- When increasing technology business in private sector there must be an increase in law and policy to protect public and private sector from victimization.

Opportunity

- Partnering with United States higher education institutions that offer online degree programs in cybersecurity, information security, information systems management, information technology, cloud computing, and machine learning.
- Building global alliances that enables citizens to acquire accredited, reliable awareness training to become knowledgeable of all cyber-domains (i.e., land, space, air, and sea).
- Increasing identity theft laws and policy.
- Building stronger alliances with global marketing and business management service providers who can be instrumental in rendering services to Rwanda to increase its citizens knowledge that can increase economic stability.
- Relying on solar panels to increase access to electricity but with increased security policy and law implementation.

- Enacting laws that protect cashless payment transactions from exploitation.
- Building alliances with global PC manufacturers to provide access to bulk purchasing.

Threats

- Government transactions online must include increased laws and policy that enforce security compliance.
- Not stressing enough that citizens access to the Internet must require increased law and policy as well as, neglecting to acknowledge that workforce support must be rendered effectively to secure citizens while connected to the Internet and while offline for personal data at rest.
- Unsecure digital ID databases.
- Lacking knowledge regarding updates of apps that are not effectively developed, managed, and secured enables an ease of access to exploitation of sensitive data sources.
- Not being aware that cashless payment systems embody vulnerabilities and pose a threat to citizens personal finance information.
- Neglecting to integrate WIFI laws and policy.
- Neglecting to integrate Internet laws and policy.
- Neglecting to audit all technology service providers, especially financial institutions and health and medical institutions to assure privacy protection of citizens data.
- Neglecting to adopt international laws and policy that govern privacy of medical and health data (i.e., HIPAA).
- Neglecting to adopt international standards for all broadband, WIFI, and Internet connections (i.e., NIST SP-800 Series publications, ISO 270001, Sarbanes Oxley, and Cloud Security).
- Neglecting to enforce back-up of all public and private information systems, mobile technology, and computerized databases.
- Neglecting to focus on increased usage of encryption on all public and private information systems and Web sites.

Mirroring international laws and policy to increase protection and enhance laws and policy within Rwanda should be a normal approach to installing effective governance methodologies. Globalized legal and policy adoption has become a normal way of increasing country's ability to defend and deter cyber-incidences. Effectively modifying international laws and policy to align with the needs of Rwanda can decrease the need to hire, train, and manage a workforce who the Rwanda government will need to enforce compliance to effectively develop and implement and/or update such law and policy as needed annually.

One of the best methods being deployed globally is effective research. Delegating a team of subject experts who can conduct efficient research to compile laws, policy, and regulatory to govern Rwanda's information systems, information databases, cloud SaaS, PaaS, and IaaS, artificial intelligence, and machine learning, will help manage how this research is modified and applied to Rwanda's law and policy needs, to protect these technology tools and systems.

The United States and the EU Commission have enacted laws and policy that should be instrumental in helping, Rwanda increase risk management over the deployment of effective cybersecurity deterrence. Furthermore, it is important to increase the education and training of citizens. Due to the low-level of educational programming currently enacted within the country, outsourcing education can be beneficial. Working with higher learning institutions within the United States and United Kingdom, can be instrumental. E-Learning programs have become a gateway to enable the world to access accredited education at low cost. Thus, deploying research on these institutional opportunities should be a priority to help accelerate accessibility and increase the level of knowledgeable and trained workforce personnel.

Samoa

Population: 199,952 * Worldometer - real time world statistics (worldometers.info)
Samoa National Cyber Security Strategy[33]
Year of publication: 2016–2021
Number of pages: 16

Strengths

- Acknowledging that cybersecurity is a shared responsibility and that endorsers are valuable assets to regulating and deterring cyber-incidences.
- Increasing global relationships.
- Increasing business awareness with cybersecurity.
- Increasing individuals' ability to be aware of cybersecurity threats and vulnerabilities.
- Increasing education of cybersecurity.

Weaknesses

- In 2021, your NCSS (National Cyber Security Strategy) "anticipates" citizens will become aware of cyber-threats and are empowered to exist safely in this digital era.
- There is a lack of public/private communication of information sharing regarding cyber-incidences.
- There is a low response to cyber-incidences.
- There is a lack of focus on effectively securing all cyber-domains (i.e., land, air, sea, and space).
- There is currently a low-level of effective technical measures (ethics and standards) to deter cyber-threats and cyber-incidences.

Opportunities

- Increasing funding resources (i.e., grants, scholarships, and loans) that enable both public/private sector to acquire access to reliable, accredited awareness education and training that increases defense methodologies to deter and reduce successful cyber-incidences and cyber related crimes.
- Increase local domestic business knowledge of encryption methodologies to effectively secure all business related financial and commercial payment processing systems and databases that host sensitive, valuable information assets.

- Build stronger global defense communication with international governments, Parliaments, and Ministries to increase globalized deterrence, laws, regulatory, and policy.
- Increasing both the Samoa cyber and Internet security frameworks.
- Integrating laws enacted by the United States, NATO, the EU Commission, and the UN can be vital assets to control standardizations of effective, efficient, and reliable laws, regulatory, and policy that enables, Samoa government to become a defense environment to fear, due to the increased penalties enacted to secure the country and decrease its cyber-incidences.
- Enhancing cooperation and response to globalized cyber-incidences and deterrence methods.
- Establishing a domestic cyber-incidence reporting system.
- Enhancing the knowledge of the National ICT Steering Committee and all stakeholders responsible for prioritizing cybersecurity mandates.
- Working effectively with all stakeholders (i.e., government, business entities, academic institutions, and organizations) to develop a culture of cybersecurity practitioners.

Like other countries, there is an obvious neglect to develop effective policy, law, and regulation that governs all cyber-domains - i.e., land, air, sea, and space. It is common to focus primarily on cyberspace because it is a general focus in most countries cybersecurity policy. However, with the increased knowledge cybercriminals have access to, to defeat their deployment of effective and strategic attack methodologies. Defining policy, law, and regulatory that defines strategies to deter their efforts in all domains - i.e., land, air, sea, and space will enable Samoa to gain control over the current trends being deployed to attack the country.

One beneficial method is increasing education and awareness training. Furthermore, it is important to increase research on global law, regulatory, and policy for international methods of deterrence. In fact, the GDPR is an essential tool that was introduced to help countries redefine strategies to protect citizens data. Also, connecting with cybersecurity policy organizations specializing in research of global cyber strategies, can be helpful too. For example, The Center of Strategic and International Studies provides a detailed research list of regulatory, including national security, military, content, privacy, critical infrastructure, commerce, and crime. Building bridges with international governments, organizations, Parliaments, Ministries, and academic institutions of higher learning offering e-learning programming that specialize in accredited education and certification programming, is another support system that can increase the knowledge of your government and the citizens of Samoa.

Singapore

Population: 5,904,522 * Worldometer - real time world statistics (worldometers.info)
Singapore's Cybersecurity Strategy[34]
Year of publication: 2016
Number of pages: 47

Strengths

- Acknowledging that reliance on information communication technologies makes Singapore vulnerable.
- Asking existing cybersecurity professionals to deepen their skills.
- Acknowledging that the Singapore government cannot achieve impenetrable systems alone.
- Acknowledging that businesses are responsible for protecting customer's personal data.
- Establishing the Cybersecurity Agency of Singapore.
- Acknowledging the value of international connectivity deterrence methodologies.
- Willfully educating and training cybersecurity workforce.
- Establishing a 4-pillar approach to cybersecurity resilience.
- Deploying the Cybersecurity Act.
- Establishing the Cybercrime Command.

Weaknesses

- Neglecting to effectively secure the global payment systems with Security Socket Layer (SSL) encryption.
- Neglecting to prepare effective risk management strategies for all domains of cyber warfare (i.e., land, air, sea, and space).
- Requiring CII owners and operators to take responsibility for securing their systems and networks, without establishing standardized auditing procedures and practices, and without increasing penalties for noncompliance, enables ineffective results.
- Neglecting to increase encryption layered security on government and public sector information systems.

Opportunities

- Enhancing the Smart Nation and sharing it globally to support global citizenship.
- Enhancing laws and penalties that hold financial institutions accountable for neglecting to effectively align information security policy with government information security and information systems cybersecurity policy and law.
- Enhancing penalties for financial institutions for neglecting to effectively increase data storage security, including enhancing encryption on data at rest and in transmission.
- When utilizing automation software, it is essential to ensure manufacturers are developing and managing these applications within the C.I.A. Triad.
- To minimize the loss of citizens' data, it is necessary to assure all CII operators and owners maintain updated databases that align storage and usability accessibility policy with international standards.
- Developing, implementing, and managing government automation and artificial intelligence SDK i.e., Software

Development Kits, to reduce vulnerabilities and decrease potential threats. Doing so will enable the government to increase penalties and fines on those found in violation of government laws, regulatory, and policy, when tampering with government automation and artificial intelligence systems.
- Imposing fines on Internet Service Providers (ISPs) for neglecting to protect the privacy and data sources of consumers, domestically and internationally.

Threats

- ISPs failing to adhere to the Secure & Resilient Internet Infrastructure Code of Practice.
- Neglecting to hold anti-virus software developer service providers accountable for not effectively securing consumers data and devices.
- Neglecting to increase cybersecurity awareness training and education for the public sector to become knowledgeable and capable of joining the public and private workforce.

Singapore is an international financial conglomerate that hosts trillions of dollars in global economic stability. Neglecting to require financial institutions to enhance the data security on data at rest and in transmission will impact the ability to effectively deter successful cybercrimes from occurring. Utilizing intrusion detection and prevention software should be mandatory for all governments, businesses, organizations, and institutions that compile, store, and share personal information of citizens, including their names, addresses, phone numbers, date of birth, and any other identifiable information that can be sold on the black market for monetary gain.

The EU, UN, and NATO have enacted laws that increase penalties for cybercriminals who engage in nefarious activities that involve financial institutions. Integrating these laws within the framework of Singapore's legal framework, can be instrumental in managing how cybercrimes are dealt with and penalized within and outside the country. In fact, Thailand recently enacted laws under Section 17 that enable persons committing an offense against Thailand outside the Kingdom, who are Thai or not, to be held accountable and penalized within the Kingdom. Adopting this approach can be a gateway to effectively manage how cybercriminals are dealt with and penalized for targeting government information systems.

It is also invaluable to increase the awareness and training of citizens within the country, on how to effectively protect their personal data, including their information communication technologies. Without clarity on how to effectively deploy security methods to prevent their mobile devices from being targeted. Or, how to configure settings within their Web browsers from enabling international cybercriminals from gaining control and access of their history files, can leave citizens vulnerable to attack. Thus, it is essential to increase funding for colleges, universities, and elementary school students to gain the knowledge and hands-on skills and training to be essential in protecting the country from victimization.

Slovakia

Population: 5,462,752 * Worldometer - real time world statistics (worldometers.info)
National Strategy for Information Security in the Slovak Republic[35]
Year of publication: 2021–2025
Number of pages: 32

Strengths

- Acknowledging the significance of information security and the importance of upgrading in specific fields.
- Acknowledging the correlation of information security and the establishment of primary legislative rules.
- Ensuring the protection of data leakage and unauthorized usage.
- Protecting citizens right to protect their personal data.
- Protecting against misuse of data and communicating systems.
- Knowing that inaccurate data protection and communication technologies raises doubts about reliability.

- Having a genuine concern of Slovakia's creditability abroad.
- Acknowledging that ensuring information security of a country is essential to the functioning of society.
- Understanding that information security is multilateral and must consider interest of ICT system owners, users, and the rights of the natural and legal persons whose data is processed and stored by such systems.
- Abiding by C.I.A. Triad.
- Understanding that information communication technology systems and data processed by such systems is often developed disfunctionally due to natural factors, technical failures, human error, malicious software, and international terrorism.
- Knowing that email possess a risk to information sharing.

Weaknesses

- Declaring the absence of a comprehensive information security strategy.
- Lacking the expert capacity and material resources to effectively meet tasks arising under a full membership.
- Lacking a clear path to data retrieval from globalized legislation regarding current trends in law, regulatory, and policy on pertinent security subject matter, engulfing information security, information systems, artificial intelligence, 3D printing, quantum computing, cloud computing, and the Internet of Things.

Opportunities

- Increasing the development of a research center that focuses on laws, regulatory, and policy encompassing information systems security, cloud computing security, information security, information technology security, artificial intelligence, machine learning, and quantum computing.

- Establishing alliances with cooperative international academic institutions who delivers accredited education programming for undergraduate and graduate degrees and certification programs for information systems, cloud infrastructure, information technology, information systems, artificial intelligence, and quantum computing.
- Enhancing citizens awareness of all cyber-incidence methodologies and security methodologies to learn how to effectively protect their information assets.
- Developing, enacting, implementing, managing, and updating legislative, regulatory, and policy on information security, information systems management, information technology, cloud infrastructure, and artificial intelligence, is essential to gaining control over the deployment of cyber-incidences domestically and internationally.
- Adopting international information security, information systems management, and cloud infrastructure laws, regulatory, and policy that enhances the knowledge and compliance of Slovakia's citizens', both public and private sectors.
- Establishing a point of contact to govern domestic and international information security incidence.

Threats

- There is a limited number of skilled, knowledgeable, and educated citizens to support the defense strategies needed to effectively secure and deter cyber-incidences engulfing information security exploitation.
- There is a lack of research and clarity on all international standards delivered as open-source documents, provided by all cooperating countries, who willfully share their laws, regulatory, and policy on matters relative to information security, information systems management, cloud computing architecture, artificial intelligence, machine learning, quantum computing, and information security.

- There is a lack of research experts to enhance knowledge and information databases on all countries laws, regulatory, and policy that can help guide the development, implementation, and management of secure ICT environments.
- There is a limited level of education and training for public and private sector citizens needed to be instrumental in protecting information assets from exploitation.

Defining clearly conveyed law, regulatory, and policy that effectively aligns with current trends in cybersecurity, information security, and information communication technologies, is a daunting task when there is a limited number of supporting citizens who can be beneficial in helping compile research and develop laws, regulatory, and policy. To combat this, it is recommended to build stronger alliances with countries that share their data on laws, regulatory, and policy regarding subject matter - i.e., information asset security and the technology tools and systems relied upon to develop, transmit, and/or store data.

It is also important to increase education and awareness training. Adopting education and training material from global governments, Parliaments, and Ministries can be a useful approach to defining effectively written learning instruction and curriculum that enhances citizens knowledge of important information security methods, practices, and procedures. Also, building alliances with globalized e-learning academic institutions of higher learning and certificate programming, may also be beneficial.

With the increased volume of cyber-incidences, increasing penalties for those deploying cyberattacks, is a sure deterrence model that other countries are utilizing and relying on. Neglecting to do so can leave open a gateway of exploitation. Building alliances with governments who are interested in working closely with countries struggling to deal with deterrence and cyber-incidences, can build bridges and reduce victimization. Otherwise, there remains a gateway for cybercriminals to succeed, which can be costly to the economy of the country.

South Africa

Population: 60,200,777 * Worldometer - real time world statistics (worldometers.info)
National Cybersecurity Policy Framework[36]
Year of publication: 2015
Number of pages: 30

Strengths

- Acknowledging the C.I.A. Triad.
- Effectively developing and implementing coherent and integrated cybersecurity approaches to address cyber-incidences.
- Establishing the Justice Crime Prevention Security Cluster who manages the JCPS Cybersecurity Response Committee to identify and priorities areas of intervention.
- Establishing the Cybersecurity Hub to be housed within the Department of Telecommunications and Postal Services.
- Acknowledging that focus needs to include strategies to deter cybercrime, cyber warfare, and cyber-terrorism.
- Ensuring a comprehensive legal framework governing cyberspace.
- Building trust and confidence in the secure use of ICT (Information Communication Technologies).
- Acknowledging that malware is being distributed via terrorist groups.
- Ensuring a swift recovery of critical information systems.
- Enhancing international cooperation.
- Promoting fundamental rights of all South Africa citizens privacy, security, dignity, access to information, right to communication, and freedom of expression.
- Understanding the importance of public/private sector communication and data sharing to address and reduce benefits to cyber criminals.

Weaknesses

- Promoting a cybersecurity culture and compliance with minimum security standards.
- There is a lack of legal and regulatory framework encompassing information systems, information security, cloud security, and Internet of Things.
- Neglecting to create trust building initiatives in domestic information communication technologies.
- Neglecting to utilize legal, regulatory, and policy governance methods to secure public and private information systems, cloud computing architecture, artificial intelligence, machine learning, learning management systems, and quantum computing, to enhance security compliance with private and public sectors.
- Neglecting to partner with international universities who delivers reliable, trusted, accredited cybersecurity, information security, information systems security, and cloud computing architecture, undergrad and graduate programming, as well as certificate programming that increases citizens' knowledge, skills, and training on these subject matters.
- Neglecting to hold international computer and software manufacturer's accountable to international standards, such as product Service License Agreement and Service Level Agreement documentation, and the United States Regulations, Laws and Information by Product for Manufacturers, Importers, Distributors, and Retailers defined by the United States Consumer Product Safety Commission.
- Failing to enact audit procedures for usage of all technology tools and systems, as well as software for public and private sector.

Opportunities

- Developing critical information infrastructure internally that increases innovation of software, learning management systems, hardware, and computer and mobile devices.

- Utilizing the GDPR (General Data Protection Regulation) is an opportunity to define, implement, and manage information security within South Africa.
- Relying on the Memorandum of Understanding as a framework for compliance.
- Updating all legislation annually or as needed (i.e., Electronic Communication & Transaction Act (2002), Electronic Communications Security LTD Act (2002), Regulation of Interception of Communication & Provision of Communication Related Information Act (2002), State Information Technology Agency Act (1998), and the Cryptographic Regulations (2006)).
- Adopting international Cryptography Regulatory legislation and policy (i.e., The Organization for Economic Cooperation and Development Cryptography Policy Guidelines).

Threats

- There is a lack of focus on securing cloud infrastructure.
- There is a lack of focus on securing artificial intelligence.
- There is a lack of focus on securing 3D printing.
- There is a lack of focus on securing Webpages and Web sites with SSL.
- There is a lack of focus on securing financial institution's Web interfaces for payment transactions.
- There is a lack of auditing procedures and compliance regulation for private and public sectors.
- There is a lack of effective education and training across all sectors to remain up to date on all cyber trends and incidences globally.
- There is neglect to increase regulation and policy to secure all cyber-domains (i.e., land, air, sea, and space).

Belgium, Canada, Denmark, France, Netherlands, and United Kingdom share laws encompassing cryptography usage, such as, Belgium's wiretap law. However, Denmark has its IT Council who currently limits citizens right to cryptography security. Having clarity on what laws, regulatory, and policy is currently available can be instrumental in helping South Africa deploy its own effective approach to governing its information systems, cloud computing architectures, artificial intelligence, machine learning, 3D printing, quantum computing, and Internet of Things.

Effective research is essential to staying up to date on current trends of cyber-incidences. It is important to work with international governments, Parliaments, and Ministries to have access to resources, laws, regulatory, and policy that will help secure the country and its citizens from being victims of cyber-incidences. Most importantly, increasing the education and training of citizens is vital to protecting, both public and private sector from unauthorized access to information assets that govern the country's economy.

Switzerland

Population: 8,730,195 * Worldometer - real time world statistics (worldometers.info)
National Strategy for the Protection of Switzerland Against Cyber Risk[37]
Year of publication: 2018–2022
Number of pages: 32

Strengths

- Acknowledging that complete protection against cyber risks cannot be achieved with proportionate measures.
- Effectively updating the National Cybersecurity Strategy from 2012 to 2022.
- Acknowledging that private sector has a role in partnering with the public sector to deploy effective cybersecurity deterrence.
- Effectively assessing past, current, and future threat situations to implement risk management strategies to deter successful cyberattacks.

- Distinguishing between what is an international unauthorized act or threat from unintentional events.
- Being knowledgeable that cyber espionage is often carried out by state and non-state actors.
- Acknowledging that vulnerabilities are often enveloped in ICT producers' products and services.
- Understanding that the Internet of Things is a gateway for cyber sabotage and cyber-terrorism.
- Acknowledging that cyber-risk due to human error will remain very significant.
- Building stronger cooperation with third parties invokes an ease of information exchange.
- Aware that aligning with "status quo" is not sufficient to ensure an adequate level of protection.
- The proposed visionary strategic objectives outlined in the NCS 2018–2022 are effective methodologies to pursue to ensure safeguarding Switzerland's citizens and ICT.
- Forecasting spheres of action and measures of the NCS 2018–2022.

Weaknesses

- There is a lack of willfully trained, skilled, and educated personnel interested in partnering with the public sector to effectively safeguard the private sector.
- Neglecting to hold financial institutions accountable for the information assets stored in non-secured information systems and databases.
- Neglecting to require increased security encryption on financial service providers Web sites and payment transmission service systems.
- Limiting prosecution on how long cybercrimes can be prosecuted.
- Ineffectively tracking cyber actors globally can impact economic stability that cripples the financial institutions' ability to rebuild trust in consumers, especially if successful cyberattacks impact the reputation of such financial institutions.

Opportunities

- Developing a cyber incident reporting terminal to compile information that can be instrumental in defining effective risk management strategies.
- Increasing cyber risk innovation solutions that private sector can utilize to increase the volume of qualified service practitioners.
- Increasing marketing and advertising strategies to increase citizens' awareness about cybersecurity that will encourage workforce personnel to become active in helping protect the country from cybercriminals.
- Building stronger alliances with international governments to gain knowledge of all methodologies being enacted and deployed to deter successful cyber-incidences.
- Increasing laws and policy that enhance prosecution of cyber-criminals domestically and internationally.

Threats

- Neglecting to secure all cyber-domains (i.e., sea, land, air, and space).
- Neglecting to effectively implement security models to secure all ICT (i.e., information technology, information systems, software, Web sites, cloud environments, artificial intelligence, 3D printing, and quantum computing).
- Ineffectively characterizing private sector cyber incident risk management methodologies can result in increased cyber-incidences that impact both public and private sectors.

The current level of qualified workforce personnel trained and educated in deterring cyber-incidences, impacts the ability to effectively safeguard the country from external cyberattack agents who continues gaining knowledge of the vulnerabilities encapsulated within the information systems relied upon across the business and government sectors. This requires an increased effort to implement encryption security on all information systems, particularly, financial institution systems and government systems. Protecting these systems is vital to securing all sensitive data traditionally stored on these technology systems. A best method is to implement reliance upon cloud environments - i.e., SaaS, IaaS, or PaaS. Doing so will help reduce the threats associated with penetrable information systems and vulnerabilities woven into software.

It is also important to increase citizens' awareness of cyber-incidences and encourage their active role in defending the country and their personal information assets from unauthorized users. This must be consistent! Otherwise, citizens will continue being victimized and their data will be sold on black markets to the highest bidder.

The growing innovation of software for Internet of Things, artificial intelligence, and quantum computing, requires increased policy to enforce security compliance and storage risk management methodologies. Without such, there is a threat of non-compliance that will leave the country vulnerable to cyber-incidences. Working with global governments to learn what is being deployed internationally, will enable Switzerland to remain current in trends and safeguard the sensitive information systems that regulate and empower the financial market.

Thailand

Population: 70,016,410 * Worldometer - real time world statistics (worldometers.info)
Enhancing Cyber Security for Government in Thailand
The National Security Policy and Plan[38]
Year of publications: 2013–2022
Number of pages: 55 and 44

Strengths

- Aligning the National Security Policy and Plan on cybersecurity with the methods deployed in Policy 10.
- Maintaining statistics and having it readily available on Internet, broadband, and disseminated to mobile phone subscribers.

- Focusing on increasing public awareness of cybercrime threats.
- Having a willingness to overcome the challenges of domestic and international cross border cooperation.
- Establishing the Computer Crime Committee.
- Establishing the National Cyber Security Committee.
- Establishing the Electronic Transaction Committee.
- Enacting the Personal Data Protection Act in 2019.
- Enacting the Cybersecurity Act.
- Empowering the Ministry of ICT to oversee the development, implementation, and management of ICT security policy.
- Establishing the Cybersecurity Operation Centre.
- Operating and providing Government Information Network Services.
- Promoting Cybersecurity Awareness.
- Establishing the ThaiCERT as the computer incident response handler.
- Enacting under Thailand Law Section 17, that any person committing an offense against the Thailand Law outside of the Kingdom, either Thai or not, will be held accountable and penalized within the Kingdom.
- Requiring the ISP to maintain traffic logs for a minimum of 90 days.
- Protecting privacy rights.
- Establishing G-Cloud.
- Establishing Cyber Scouts.
- Relying on U.S. policy strategies (i.e., NIST, ISO 270001/ 270002, COBIT).

Weaknesses

- Ineffectively deploying increased usage of security software for computer information systems of public sector, while neglecting to encourage private sector to adopt identical methodologies.

- Insufficient law enforcement experts in cybersecurity.
- The 2012 percentage of information gathering cyber-threats was compiled at 7.9% and 7.8% in 2021. This threat remains and requires increased strategic risk management planning to effectively decrease these statistics in coming years.
- The 2012 percentage of intrusion crimes were recorded at 1.7% and rose to 20.8% in 2021.
- There has been an increase of information security vulnerabilities within the public sector since 2012.
- Neglecting to increase the IoT security models (i.e., default settings modified with increased password modifications and authentication log-in).
- There has been a recorded increase of 30.1% security vulnerabilities impacting the public and private sector since 2012.
- Neglecting to increase research efforts on reliable security methodologies being deployed globally.

Opportunities

- Utilizing the statistics compiled by the ThaiCERT on the type of threats to deploy increased security methodologies for each type of threat (i.e., Internet fraud, Internet information gathering, intrusion attempts, and malicious code).
- Relying on intrusion detecting software to decrease the number of intrusion attempts (i.e., SNORT, ZEEK, OSSEC, and SECURITY ONION).
- Deploying increased malware protection software and Transport Layer Security.
- Enhancing cybersecurity methods and policy across all industries (i.e., energy, health, transportation, financial, ICT, water, food, public and legal order, and safety, chemical and nuclear industry, as well as space and research). The financial sector should be required to increase data encryption on all financial files and data resources transmitted via technology systems and tools.

- Annual auditing should be deployed to assure all information systems, cloud environments, software, and hardware security updates and vulnerability assessments align with the Government of Thailand cybersecurity policy and law.
- Enhancing penalties and fines for non-compliance on all sectors.
- Building stronger communication alliances with NATO, EU, and the UN.

Threats

- Neglecting to effectively research all ICT laws, policy, and regulatory being implemented by governments, Parliaments, and Ministries internationally.
- Failing to impose accountability requirements for all public and private sector utilizing information technology, information systems, cloud environments, software, and hardware to create, share, and store citizens personal data.
- Neglecting to require annual auditing of all ICT (i.e., information systems, cloud environments, artificial intelligence, Internet of Things, quantum computing, 3D printing, geographic information systems, and robotics).
- Neglecting to increase knowledge sharing on cyber-incidences domestically and internationally.
- Neglecting to increase education and awareness training for public and private sector, including citizens.
- Neglecting to take the initiative to build stronger alliances of communication with international governments, Parliaments, Ministries, and authorized agencies governing cybersecurity policy development, implementation, and management internationally.

With the limited number of educated, skilled, and trained workforce personnel within the geographic perimeter of Thailand, expecting 100% deterrence is challenging to attain. Thus, it is recommended to increase relationship building with international cybersecurity agencies authorized by governments, Parliaments, and Ministries who oversee the development, implementation, and managing of all cyber security policy. Focusing on each industry and the special security needs of the ICT utilized within these industries, will increase the ability to govern these environments, even with a minimum workforce. Learning to increase reliance on software automation as a service (SAaaS), infrastructure as a service (IaaS), and platforms as a service (PaaS), will require increased knowledge on these services and service providers, who can assist in helping effectively manage the vulnerabilities engulfing current information systems, software, hardware, cloud environments, artificial intelligence, quantum computing, Internet of Things, 3D printing, and robotics. Thus, relying on research provided by these industry system service providers who can help deploy and manage these systems, will also help decrease the need to rely on workforce personnel that doesn't exists. However, when working with these system service providers, it is crucial that current workforce personnel is maintaining their training of these systems and aligning their auditing efforts with these system service providers recommendations and international government, Parliaments, and Ministries recommendations. Otherwise, the impact of catastrophic incidence within these systems can be costly.

Thus, working with international governments, Parliaments, and Ministries, as well as authorized agencies who oversee cybersecurity policy development, implementation, and management, will continue being the best approach to staying current with trends enveloping all ICT, including cloud environments. Therefore, please recommend to the Cybersecurity Operation Center, to increase its efforts to compile global research on all industry ICT. Doing so will increase the knowledge of the best methods of securing these ICTs within these industries and decrease the impact of current trends in cyber-incidences.

Trinidad & Tobago

Population: 1,404,960 * Worldometer - real time world statistics (worldometers.info)
National Cybersecurity Strategy[39]
Year of publication: 2012
Number of pages: 29

Strengths

- Drafting the 2018–2022 National ICT Plans as a key component to safeguard public/private technology tools, systems, and environments.
- Acknowledging that ineffective mitigation and management of ICT's can have a deleterious effect on the reputation of the Government of Trinidad & Tobago, domestically and internationally.
- Deploying strategies that protect the physical, virtual, and intellectual assets of citizens and organizations through the development of an effective mechanism, which focuses on and responds to all cyber-threats.
- Promoting awareness to all citizens to increase cyber risk awareness and to invite citizens to become deterrence agents in the war against cyber-incidences.
- Deploying effective incident management measures that respond to initial attack damage and reduces the impact of catastrophic incidences.
- Relying on a legal framework that is efficient and effective in deterring cyber risk and successful cyber-incidences.
- Thriving to improve connectivity.
- Increasing human capacity.
- Fostering economic development.
- Clearly conveying (5) key areas (i.e., governance, incident management, collaboration, culture, and legislation) as primary components to effectively safeguard the country and citizens from victimization of cyber-incidences.
- Introducing legislation relating to ICT-related laws and policies.
- Recognizing the value of ICT and the establishment of a diversified knowledge economy, has on defining framework for sustainable development.
- Acknowledging underserved communities and their need to engage with the world via ICT.
- Understanding the value of effective communication and data sharing.
- Adhering to the C.I.A. Triad.

- Researching the expected Vision 2020 in the Fast Forward 2003–2008 National ICT plan.
- Increasing a forecast of strategic planning that fosters effective outcomes to deter continued growth of cyber deterrence shared between the community, schools, and the government.
- Thriving to be a knowledge-based economy.
- Establishing the Trinidad & Tobago Cybersecurity Agency.

Weaknesses

- Neglecting to enact cybercrime laws to deter global cyberattacks.
- Limited security policy governing broadband usage and services.
- Ineffectively holding broadband service providers accountable for securing citizens connections.
- Limiting review to the third year could be an enabler for exploitation prior to the 3rd year review of the NICT Plan.
- Neglecting to encompass all cyber-domains (i.e., land. air, sea, and space) in the National Cybersecurity Strategy.
- Neglecting to focus on all information technology components as gateways for unauthorized intrusion (i.e., malicious software and free mobile application downloads).
- Neglecting to consider all cyber-incidences as potential threats to Trinidad & Tobago (i.e., cyber warfare, cyber-terrorism, cyber stalking, cyber-espionage, and cyberbullying).
- Conducting periodic review of standards, policies, and regulations that should be done annually.

Opportunities

- Enacting legal and regulatory framework that increases penalties for cyber-incidences deployed externally.
- Increasing extradition of cybercriminals domestically and internationally.

- Building stronger alliances with international governments to gain leverage over cyber criminals and current trends in cybercrime.
- Having a predetermined outline of critical systems and methods of mitigating vulnerabilities prior to exploitation of such critical systems.
- Increasing innovation of security software and secure applets for mobile usage.

Threats

- Neglecting to hold Internet Service Providers (ISP) accountable to international standards of information security, information systems management security, cloud environments, artificial intelligence, Internet of Things, quantum computing, and mobile applications.
- Neglecting to require financial institutions to implement increased security of banking transmission services to secure sensitive data.
- Neglecting to increase citizens awareness of their role and responsibilities to safeguard their personal information assets.
- Neglecting to increase academic programming that effectively educates and prepares a growing workforce to protect the country from international cyber-incidences.

With an increased reliance upon broadband services, there must be an increase of law and policy enacted to increase requirements of broadband service providers. Accountability is essential when rendering private sector enterprises power to regulate and manage the sensitive information consumers create, transmit, and store on mobile devices. When service providers are not held accountable, the increase of human error bridges the gap of entrance to exploit vulnerable systems that house sensitive data. This can lead to catastrophic incidences that increase cost and impact economic stability.

Taking an active role in gaining clarity of global governments approach to enact and deploy information security policy and law that governs broadband and Internet services, can help decrease the threat of inefficient knowledge. Furthermore, it is important to increase cyber incident knowledge programming delivered via academic institutions - i.e., elementary, secondary, post-secondary, and higher education. Relying on these institutional systems curriculum and instructional training programs to prepare the future workforce to understand how to effectively safeguard and protect the country and its information systems from vulnerabilities and international cyberattack agents, is crucial to maintaining a secure country cyber environment. Neglecting to do so can be costly.

Thus, it is suggested to research International Internet Laws as a source of guidance to enact law, regulatory, and policy that aligns with standards to regulate how ISPs within the country, deploy effective information security. Researching regulatory groups, such as, Internet Governance Forum, Global Commission on Internet Names and Numbers, and the United Nations Commission on International Trade Laws, will be instrumental in helping effectively deploy methods of security that decreases successful cyber-incidences.

Uganda

Population: 47,587,409 * Worldometer - real time world statistics (worldometers.info)
National Information Security Policy[40]
Year of publication: 2014
Number of pages: 51

Strengths

- Enforcing the National Information Security Policy as a mandatory tool to safeguard and educate both public and private sector on their roles and responsibilities to secure all information assets.
- Relying on the International Telecommunication Union and their definition of critical infrastructure to define an effective approach to address all aspects of governance of information, personnel, and physical security.
- Requiring the review and necessary modifications to remain current with information security trends, annually.

- Stressing that the National Information Security Policy of 2014 was a baseline security control.
- Acknowledging that organizations must deploy increased effort beyond baseline security control recommendations to remain impenetrable.
- Recommending the creation of a National Information Security Advisory Group to advise the GoU on information security governance matters.
- Establishing the National Computer Emergency Response Team.
- Delegating senior personnel accountable for information security.
- Personnel accountability.
- Requiring suitable security controls to secure all data transmission "regardless" of transfer methods.
- Adopting the U.S. ISO 270001 standards.
- Requiring business organization boards to choose a designated information risk owner and be accountable for information assets.
- Requiring business continuity and disaster recovery planning be defined, implemented, and managed across all organizational environments utilizing and relying on information assets.
- Requiring consistent testing, auditing, and updating of business continuity plans regularly to ensure their effectiveness in the event of an emergency.
- Requiring all assessments and auditing reports be provided to Boards quarterly conveying a consistency in deploying effective mitigation efforts, if an emergency arise.

Weaknesses

- Only aligning compliance with information security policy with U.S. ISO/IEC 27001.
- Neglecting to align information security policy requirements with all computing systems (i.e., artificial intelligence,

Internet of Things, quantum computing, cloud environments, and robotics).

- Neglecting to impose strict security control configurations on Web browsers to enable citizens secure usage of such.
- Neglecting to enact policy that requires effective configuration of all default settings on technology tools, systems, and peripherals to enhance security.

Opportunities

- Enacting policy and law that holds globally distributed ICT service providers accountable for known heightened systems and software risks.
- Increasing education and awareness training on how to effectively secure ICT tools, including computers, information systems, cloud environments, artificial intelligence, quantum computing, robotics, and Internet of Things.
- Building stronger alliances with global governments, Parliaments, and Ministries to remain current with cyber-incidences and penalties for violators of cyber laws and policy.

Threats

- There is a minimum focus to effectively deploy security measures to deter penetration of information systems, cloud environments, artificial intelligence, and Internet of Things.
- There is a lack of security encompassing other cyber-domains (i.e., sea, space, and air).
- Neglecting to align current laws and policy encompassing information security, cyber security, cloud security, artificial intelligence security, Internet of Things security, quantum computing security, with NATO and EU International information security policy, cloud security policy, A.I. security policy, and IoT security policy.

There is a growing effort to deter cyber-incidences, but the growing number of cyberattack agents is continuing to out rank the deployment of deterrence methods currently implemented internationally. Thus, the need to partner with international governments, Parliaments, Ministries, and academic institutions increases as a method of gaining knowledge and sharing knowledge on what methodologies are currently being implemented to increase deterrence strategies and decrease successful attack methods. Cybersecurity policy is a secondary approach to managing and deterring cyber-threats, vulnerability exploitation, and cybercriminals from targeting territories that are not effectively secured. To remain current requires adopting policy strategies from globalized governments, Parliaments, and Ministries who are managing well knowledgeable teams of professionals and experts, who continues conducting effective research that enables these constituencies to build stronger deterrence models that help safeguard their sensitive information assets and ICTs. Otherwise, the battle to win becomes isolated and prevents effectiveness to rule.

Furthermore, it is invaluable to continue training current personnel on their role and responsibilities to safeguard the work environments they manage, as well as increase end-user knowledge that enables all Uganda workforce personnel, to have clarity on what steps should be implemented to keep the technology tools relied upon secure from external attack agents, who often penetrate the firewalls and security methods implemented, but are not effectively implemented to prevent successful entrance into these technology tools and system gateways.

United Arab Emirates

Population: 10,036,566 * Worldometer - real time world statistics (worldometers.info)
National Security Strategy[41]
Year of publication: 2017–2019
Number of pages: 28

Strengths

- Acknowledging that cybersecurity incidents extend beyond economic losses that impact direct financial impact, client impact, impact on services, and reputational impact.

- Leveraging the National Cybersecurity Strategy on three key sources of insight: globalized industry reports, partnering with cybersecurity experts, and building alliances with 10 benchmark countries.
- Fostering a culture of entrepreneurship in cybersecurity.
- Enacting five pillars that aspire to mobilize the whole ecosystem.
- Encouraging professionals and students to pursue a career in cybersecurity.

Weaknesses

- Limiting the scope of technologies to effectively secure cloud computing, artificial intelligence, Internet of Things, quantum computing, and robotics, which should all be encompassed within the scope of securing emerging and existing technologies.
- There is a lack of globalized cyber incident information sharing.
- Neglecting to align aspired CIIP program "world-class" risk management standards with international standards (i.e., ISO 27001, ISO 27002, NIST, HIPAA, Cloud security, IoT security, A.I. security, quantum computing security, and robotic security models).
- Aspiring to enact legal framework to address all types of cybercrimes.
- Neglecting to provide incentives to increase citizens interest in becoming actively involved in cyber security, information technology security, cloud computing security, artificial intelligence security, quantum computing security, and Internet of Things security.

Opportunities

- Increasing the level of knowledge citizens acquire about their role and responsibility in helping deter successful cyber-incidences impacting their personal computer and mobile devices.
- Increasing incentives to encourage citizens interest in becoming educated and trained within academic institutions that provide accredited educational training and knowledge beyond undergraduate studies to pursue higher education (i.e., master and doctorate degrees).
- Establishing effective compliance regulatory and policy that aligns with global laws to protect information communication technologies (ICT) from external attack agents.
- Increasing global communication and information sharing on cyber-incidences that impact the economy of the country.

Threats

- Neglecting to partner with international governments, Parliaments, and Ministries to remain current with trends in cyber-incidences that can have catastrophic impact on economies.
- Neglecting to effectively require annual auditing of all government information systems.
- Neglecting to require financial institutions to implement increased encryption on all information systems, including banking Web sites and payment processing systems.
- Neglecting to increase penalties for cybercrimes committed domestically and internationally.
- Failing to remain compliant with international treaties encompassing cyber laws and policy that protect citizens from cyber victimization.

Aspiring to implement strategies to defeat cybercriminals is not enough to deter and prevent successful cyberattacks from impacting the economy, government, business, academic institutions, and citizens from being victimized. Effective strategies are required to decrease the success of cyberattacks deployed against vulnerable computer systems, cloud environments, robotics, artificial intelligence, quantum computing systems, and Internet of Things. Without effective security models defined and implemented with strategized risk management methods, there remains a gateway of entrance that can be costly if not secured correctly. While there is no 100% effective method to secure any software or hardware technology tool or system. There are standards that have been discussed, researched, and implemented to enable government systems from being successfully penetrated. Having clarity on these steps, strategies, regulations, and standards can help decrease the success of cyber-incidences nationally.

Additionally, it is invaluable to effectively educate citizens on the role they play in protecting their own information assets and computer systems. Having knowledge regarding what needs to be done to safeguard their personal computers and mobile devices, is a first step. Furthermore, it is important to educate and train citizens on what are the best sources for gaining increased knowledge on safeguarding their homes and the computerized systems embedded within their homes i.e., Internet of Things. Providing increased funding to academic institutions and programs that effectively educate and prepare citizens about the role and responsibilities, they have to protect themselves and their workplace ICTs, also plays a significant role in how successful the national cybersecurity strategy can be. It requires a group effort to effectively secure any environment of computer systems utilized consistently for public sector purposes. Thus, increasing the growth and aspiration of the current cyber strategies will help United Arab Emirates to remain complaint with safeguarding its information assets from external unauthorized attack agents. However, research is a vital component to continued security success.

United Kingdom

Population: 68,324,581 * Worldometer - real time world statistics (worldometers.info)
National Cybersecurity Strategy[42]
Year of publication: 2016–2021
Number of pages: 80

Strengths

- Acknowledging all cyber-domains (i.e., land, air, sea, and space).
- Thriving to protect citizens privacy.
- Developing, implementing, and managing a five-year strategy to deter cyber-incidences.
- Being aware that the discussion on cybersecurity is not something to be discussed behind closed doors.
- Being aware that cybersecurity is a threat that cannot be eliminated.
- The UK government acknowledges its responsibilities to safeguard companies, citizens, and organizations operating in the UK.
- Having an ability to support and collaborate internationally with allies and partners in the fight against cybercriminals.
- Reporting annual progress encompassing efforts deployed to secure companies, citizens, and organizations operating in the UK.
- Acknowledging that the 2011 National Cyber Strategy alone was not capable of achieving the scale and pace of change required to stay ahead of the threat of cyber-incidences.
- Enforcing international action and investing in international partnerships that shape the global evolution of cyberspace.
- Conveying in policy that cybercriminals will be brought overseas to justice.
- Acknowledging that international partnerships enhance collective security.
- Working closely with EU, NATO, and the UN both bilaterally and multilaterally.
- Thriving to filter known bad IP addresses and block malicious online activities.
- Establishing the National Cyber Security Centre as the authority on the UK's cyber security environment.
- Increasing the amount of time, effort, and funding needed to address the shortage of cybersecurity skills in the UK for schools and universities across the workforce.

- Allocating a proposition of the Defense and Cyber Innovation funding to support innovative procurement in defense and security.
- Establishing the Cyber Invest.
- Acknowledging the power of remote exploitation.
- Acknowledging that the UK Government alone cannot provide all aspects of the nation's cybersecurity.
- Understanding that fraud, theft, and extortion against the UK is financially motivated by Russian-language organized criminal groups in Eastern Europe.
- Acknowledging the skills of script-kiddies.
- Implementing case studies in the 2016–2021 National Cyber Security Strategy.

Weaknesses

- Focusing primarily on young minds as potential cybersecurity experts instead of all Age groups.
- Neglecting to implement risk management strategies that deter attacks from South Asia and West Africa through the enactment of increased penalties for all cybercrimes committed domestically and internationally.
- Increasing negotiations to enhance international laws and penalties for cybercrimes committed internationally, including extradition arrangements.
- Undermining the potential threats all state and state actors can commit against the UK Government, UK citizens, businesses, and organizations.
- The Cyber Aware Campaign does not encompass the promotion of multi-layer authentication log-in for all software systems operating in computers, mobile devices, ICTs, artificial intelligence, IoT, and cloud environments.
- Neglecting to enforce reporting of cyber-incidences between public & private sector to increase knowledge sharing and deterrence methodologies.

Opportunities

- Increasing effective promotion, advertising, and marketing of cybersecurity crime incident practices and the National Cyber Security incident reporting agency.
- Encouraging usage of software that is capable of being configured to effectively enable security methodologies to be deployed as safeguard models to decrease usage of software with known vulnerabilities.
- Campaigning to reduce access to videos and digital content online that educates anyone about how to hack into computers, information systems, artificial intelligence, quantum computing, cloud environments, and IoT (Internet of Things).
- Censoring online material that enables anyone to learn how to exploit system vulnerabilities.
- Increasing the usage of cloud environments as safeguarded technology tools for government, business, organizations, and citizens.
- Increasing usage of cybersecurity insurance as a resource to help rebuild systems and private/public sector environments impacted by catastrophic cybercrime incidences.
- Building stronger alliances with private sector to increase resilience and cyber-incidence awareness.

Threats

- Neglecting to impose heightened cybersecurity awareness training and education efforts that enhance private sector deterrence capabilities to effectively deploy risk management strategies to decrease exploitation of all ICTs, including computers, information systems, cloud environments, artificial intelligence, quantum computing, 3D printing, robotics, and IoT.
- Building security by default without effectively training end-users on how to maintain built-in security defaults.

- Neglecting to implement effective IP address security efforts that combat the implementation of subnetted IP addresses across virtual private networks.
- Neglecting to enhance penalties on crimes committed across the UK's Internet routing infrastructure.
- Lacking clarity on "all" potential malware attacks integrated in search engines (i.e., sophisticated infusion of malware websites developed and submitted to search engines).
- Neglecting to require manufacturers of software and hardware to provide instructions to end-users on how to effectively secure all software and hardware from exploitation via default settings configurations.

The continued enhancement of the National Cyber Security Strategy conveys a strategy and quest to effectively manage a country that is endlessly under attack. This requires working to build stronger alliances globally and aligning current efforts with international laws and policy that encompass cybercrime and incidences. Having clarity on what other governments, Parliaments, and Ministries are doing to deter cyber-incidences, is beneficial in modifying current trends and implementing new approaches that have not been introduced.

It is also invaluable to continue educating and training all citizens about cybercrime and cyber-incidences, and how these nefarious acts are deployed, both on land, in space, and by sea. Therefore, increasing penalties is a must. Doing so will help deter cybercriminals from targeting countries that have increased penalties for crimes committed against the country and all ICTs within the country. Working closely with international governments, Parliaments, and Ministries to enhance extradition efforts, is another approach that should not be wavered. This is a step towards increasing how all governments should respond and act when dealing with international cybercrime.

However, it is important to understand there is no 100% deterrence model that will absolutely stop every cyber incident from impacting governments, Parliaments, Ministries, and public sector industries. Thus, having standards enacted and managing the ICTs relied upon effectively and efficiently, is the best method to decreasing the number of successful cyberattacks across all industry systems. Having clarity on the software and systems relied upon across all industries, will enable effective management strategies to help control potential threats and vulnerabilities that are known and have been targeted and successful exploited. When there is an absence of clarity on what methods are being deployed globally to deter and effectively impose risk management, its leaves room for unauthorized access to systems to become easily accessible and easy to exploit.

Vietnam

Population: 98,422,301 * Worldometer - real time world statistics (worldometers.info)
Vietnamese Cybersecurity Strategy[43]
Year of publication: 2016–2020
Number of pages: 8

Strengths

- Enacting the law on Cybersecurity in 2019.
- Requiring onshore and offshore service providers to host all stored data of Vietnamese end-users in Vietnam.
- Requiring offshore entities to establish branches of representative within Vietnam territory.
- Taking the initiative to request online and offshore service providers to omit offensive digital content.
- Enabling the Ministry of Information and Communication as well as the Ministry of Public Security to conduct audit of information systems, including hardware, software, digital devices as well as transmitted, processed, and stored data.
- Establishing the Cyberspace Operations Command.

Weaknesses

- Neglecting to require wireless carrier Viettel to enhance mobile device security to protect end-users' personal data.
- Requiring tech companies to store data about Vietnamese nationals on servers in-country where access to physical

servers is prone to increased unauthorized intrusion; instead of relying on cloud environments with limited access and limited Key Pair control.

- Periodically verifying and implementing assessment of cybersecurity within the nation's information systems, software, hardware, and information technology.
- Neglecting to enhance encryption reliability of national and international electronic transaction activities towards socialization.
- Ineffectively providing cybersecurity awareness training and education to government personnel and requiring private sector do the same to align with government practices.
- Neglecting to audit government information systems for vulnerabilities annually and maintaining written and recorded logs effectively.

Opportunities

- Establishing the cybersecurity incidence reporting Centre.
- Increasing cybersecurity workforce through continued educational training in high school, college, graduate, and postgraduate programming.
- Building stronger alliances with international governments to foster effective cybersecurity and information security data sharing.
- Increasing the innovation of government software to secure all ICTs, including information systems, cloud environments, artificial intelligence, quantum computing, 3D printing, robotics, and Internet of Things.
- Foster continued relationships with private sector to increase their knowledge, awareness, and ability to deter attacks and effectively thwart known vulnerabilities from being easily exploitable.

- Investing in citizens to become instrumental cybersecurity and information security workforce personnel who takes pride in defending the country from domestic and international cyberattack agents.
- Increasing cybersecurity on political information systems with virtual private cloud services.

Threats

- Neglecting to implement clearly written usage policy that governs public sector information systems, cloud environments, artificial intelligence, Internet of Things, 3D printing, quantum computing, and all software.
- Neglecting to audit public sector information systems, cloud environments, artificial intelligence, Internet of Things, 3D printing, quantum computing, and all software annually to maintain efficient security risk management.
- Neglecting to enhance government funding to build a stronger cybersecurity workforce.
- Failing to align all cybersecurity. information systems, and information security policy with international laws and policy, to increase awareness, education, and training models for both public and private sectors.
- Neglecting to stay current with trends in cyber-incidences internationally.

Periodically deploying assessments of information systems that are crucial to daily government, business, financial, health, and academic environments and institutions, is a hazard to effectively securing the software and hardware from exploitable vulnerabilities embedded within these systems and applications. If cybercriminals can log-online to gain knowledge of how to hack new software or old hardware, having knowledge to achieve the end goal is half of the effort to achieve success in exploiting these environments and systems. Thus, it is imperative that annual auditing be deployed across all ICT

(Information Communication Technologies), to assure these systems and applications are secure. It is just as invaluable to effectively train and educate the workforce operating, managing, and overseeing risk management of these systems and applications. Neglecting to do so will result in catastrophic cyber-incidences that will increase budget spending and cost to either repair and/or integrate new systems, software, and applications. One way to minimize the vulnerabilities within systems and software, is staying current with the recommendations of the software and application manufacturers who provide updated system security methods that help decrease known vulnerabilities. Otherwise, the implementation of policy and law would be vain and useless.

It is also invaluable to stay current with global laws, regulatory, and policy regarding the systems and software relied upon within the country. Government systems should be secured and align with policies and law that enable increased penalties and fines for violators who attack these systems and software. Neglecting to align with world laws and policy encompassing these systems and software, leaves the country vulnerable.

Most importantly, building stronger alliances of communication and data sharing with governments, Parliaments, and Ministries will help decrease the concern for the lack of knowledge on how to effectively deploy risk management and mitigation strategies as needed. With the increase of innovation in software and information systems, there is a need to increase knowledge and awareness training that enables workforce and citizens to understand their role and responsibilities in managing and securing these ICTs. Effective policy development, implementation, and management requires compliance.

Summary

Each of these 43 countries have established their own approach to defining, developing, implementing, and managing cybersecurity policy. What distinguishes each country's cybersecurity public policy is the type of cyber-incidences being deployed within each territory. NATO, EU, and the UN have worked in partnership to develop effective cybersecurity public policy that can be instrumental in managing other countries information systems, information security, information technology, artificial intelligence, 3D printing, cloud environments, Internet of Things, software, hardware, and robotics. Without clearly conveyed cybersecurity public policy, compliance regulation can often be ineffective. Although laws are enacted, unless citizens and businesses are knowledgeable of these laws, these too are often ignored. This increases the risk of vulnerabilities being exploited.

The growing number of cyberattacks deployed with Ransomware, malware, viruses, worms, Trojans, and botnets, requires governments, Parliaments, and Ministries to remain diligent in understanding how these attacks are being deployed and how to safeguard systems from being victimized by these malicious technology components of warfare. Therefore, researching the vulnerabilities engulfing these software applications is a must! Neglecting to do so can be costly and impact economic stability. Most importantly, neglecting to understand how these systems are secured will increase the ability to penetrate them endlessly. While cybercriminals continue increasing knowledge and skills to gain access to vulnerable systems. It is imperative governments, Parliaments, and Ministries work together to build stronger alliances and share ideals on criminalization, increase of penalties, and methods of deterrence. Otherwise, the war on cybercrime will never be defeated.

Discussion Questions

1. Who should be held accountable to protecting citizens private data the most? Why?
2. Why should broadband service providers be held to higher standards of information security?
3. What happens when ISP and broadband service providers are not held accountable for information security?
4. What country delegated their 2014 National Information Security Policy as a baseline security control?
5. Why should Web browser security configuration be done?
6. What country leverages the National Cybersecurity Strategy on three key sources of insight?
7. What countries neglect to establish cyber incident reporting systems?

8. What country established the CyberInvest?
9. What country acknowledges the skills of script-kiddies?

Notes

1 Afghanistan, (2014). National Security Public Policy: National Cyber Security Strategy of Afghanistan. Web site: https://www.itu.int/en/ITU-D/Cybersecurity/Documents/National_Strategies_Repository/Afghanistan_2014_National%20Cybersecurity%20Strategy%20of%20Afghanistan%20%28November2014%29.pdf

2 Australia, (2020). Australia Cybersecurity Strategy. Web site: https://www.home-affairs.gov.au/cyber-security-subsite/files/cyber-security-strategy-2020.pdf

3 Bermuda, (2018). Bermuda Cybersecurity Strategy. Web site: https://www.gov.bm/sites/default/files/10999-National-Cybersecurity-Strategy.pdf

4 Canada, (2018). National Cybersecurity Strategy. Web site: https://www.public-safety.gc.ca/cnt/rsrcs/pblctns/ntnl-cbr-scrt-strtg/index-en.aspx

5 Chili, (2017). National Cybersecurity Policy. Web site: https://www.itu.int/en/ITU-D/Cybersecurity/Documents/National_Strategies_Repository/Chile_NCSP%20%28ENG%29.pdf

6 Croatia, (2015). National Cybersecurity Strategy of the Republic of Croatia. Web site: https://www.enisa.europa.eu/topics/national-cyber-security-strategies/ncss-map/CRNCSSEN.pdf

7 Cyprus, (2017). Cybersecurity Strategy of the Republic of Cyprus. Web site: https://www.newstrategycenter.ro/wp-content/uploads/2019/07/George_Michaelides_Cyber_Security_Strategy_of_RoCyprus.pdf

8 Czeck Republic, (2011). Cybersecurity Strategy of the Czeck Republic. Web site: https://www.enisa.europa.eu/media/news-items/CZ_Cyber_Security_Strategy_20112015.PDF

9 Dubai, (2017). Dubai Cybersecurity Strategy. Web site: https://www.desc.gov.ae/app/uploads/2020/05/CSS_Eng.pdf

10 Egypt, (2017). National Cybersecurity Strategy. Web site: https://www.itu.int/en/ITU-D/Cybersecurity/Documents/National_Strategies_Repository/EgyptNational%20Cybersecurity%20Strategy-English%20version-18%20Nov%202018.pdf

11 Estonia, (2014). Estonia Cybersecurity Policy. Web site: https://www.mkm.ee/sites/default/files/cyber_security_strategy_2014-2017_public_version.pdf

12 European Commission, (2020). EU Security Union Strategy. Web site: https://eur-lex.europa.eu/legal-content/EN/TXT/PDF/?uri=CELEX:52020DC0605&from=EN

13 Finland, (2019). Finland's Cyber Strategy. Web site: https://turvallisuuskomitea.fi/wp-content/uploads/2019/10/Kyberturvallisuusstrategia_A4_ENG_WEB_031019.pdf

14 Gambia, (2020). Gambia National Cybersecurity Policy, Strategies, and Action Plans. Web site: https://moici.gov.gm/sites/default/files/2021-05/CYBERSECURITY%20STRATEGY%20%26%20ACTION%20PLAN%202024.pdf

15 Germany, (2011). Cyber Strategy for Germany. Web site: https://ccdcoe.org/uploads/2018/10/Germany_cyber-security-strategy-2021_English.pdf

16 Greece, (2020). National Cybersecurity Strategy. Web site: https://www.enisa.europa.eu/topics/national-cyber-security-strategies/ncss-map/GRNCSS_EN.pdf

17 Hungary, (2013). National Cybersecurity Strategy of Hungary. Web site: https://www.enisa.europa.eu/topics/national-cyber-security-strategies/ncss-map/HU_NCSS.pdf

18 Icelandic, (2015). Icelandic National Cybersecurity Strategy. Web site: https://www.government.is/media/innanrikisraduneyti-media/media/frettir-2015/Icelandic_National_Cyber_Security_Summary_loka.pdf

19 Ireland, (2019). National Cyber Strategy. Web site: https://www.ncsc.gov.ie/pdfs/National_Cyber_Security_Strategy.pdf

20 Italy, (2013). National Strategic Framework for Cyberspace Security. Webs site: https://www.sicurezzanazionale.gov.it/sisr.nsf/wp-content/uploads/2014/02/italian-national-strategic-framework-for-cyberspace-security.pdf

21 Japan, (2017). The Cybersecurity Policy for Critical Infrastructure Protection. Web site: https://www.nisc.go.jp/eng/pdf/cs_policy_cip_eng_v4.pdf

22 Kenya, (2014). National Cybersecurity Strategy. Web site: https://www.itu.int/en/ITU-D/Cybersecurity/Documents/National_Strategies_Repository/Kenya_2014_GOK-national-cybersecurity-strategy.pdf

23 Republic of Kosovo, (2016). National Cybersecurity Strategy & Action Plan. Web site: https://kryeministri.rks-gov.net/wp-content/uploads/docs/National_Cyber_Security_Strategy_and_Action_Plan_2016-2019_per_publikim_1202.pdf

24 Kuwait, (2017). National Cybersecurity Strategy for the State of Kuwait. Web site: https://citra.gov.kw/sites/en/LegalReferences/English%20Cyber%20Security%20Strategy.pdf

25 Luxembourg, (2018). National Cybersecurity Strategy. Web site: https://hcpn.gouvernement.lu/dam-assets/fr/publications/brochure-livre/national-cybersecurity-strategy-3/national-cybersecurity-strategy-iii-en-.pdf

26 Malaysia, (n.d.). National Cybersecurity Policy. Web site: https://cnii.cybersecurity.my/main/ncsp/NCSP-Policy2.pdf

27 Nepal, (2016). National Cybersecurity Strategy. Web site: https://www.enisa.europa.eu/topics/national-cyber-security-strategies/ncss-map/national_cyber_security_strategy_2016.pdf

28 Netherland, (2018). An Integrated International Security Strategy. Web site: https://www.enisa.europa.eu/news/member-states/CSAgenda_EN.pdf

29 New Zealand, (2019). New Zealand Cybersecurity Strategy 2019. Web site: https://dpmc.govt.nz/sites/default/files/2019-07/Cyber%20Security%20Strategy.pdf

30 Norway, (2003). National Cybersecurity Strategy for Norway. Web site: https://www.regjeringen.no/contentassets/c57a0733652f47688294934ffd93fc53/national-cyber-security-strategy-for-norway.pdf

31 Poland, (2019). Cybersecurity Strategy of the Republic of Poland. Web site: https://www.enisa.europa.eu/topics/national-cyber-security-strategies/ncss-map/Cybersecuritystrategy_PL.pdf

32 Rwanda, (2019). Information Communication Technology Sector Strategic Plan. Web site: https://www.risa.rw/fileadmin/user_upload/Others%20documents/ICT4_GOV_CLUSTER_STRATEGY_2020-2024.pdf

33 Samoa, (2016). Samoa National Cybersecurity Strategy. Web site: https://www.samoagovt.ws/wp-content/uploads/2017/02/MCIT-Samoa-National-Cybersecurity-Strategy-2016-2021.pdf

34 Singapore, (2016). Singapore's Cybersecurity Strategy. Web site: https://www.csa.gov.sg/news/publications/singapore-cybersecurity-strategy

35 Slovakia, (2021). National Strategy for Information Security in the Slovak Republic. Web site: https://www.enisa.europa.eu/topics/national-cyber-security-strategies/ncss-map/Slovakia_National_Strategy_for_ISEC.pdf
36 South Africa, (2015). National Cybersecurity Policy Framework. Web site: https://www.gov.za/sites/default/files/gcis_document/201512/39475gon609.pdf
37 Switzerland, (2018). National Strategy for the Protection of Switzerland Against Cyber Risk. Web site: https://www.ncsc.admin.ch/ncsc/en/home/strategie/strategie-ncss-2018-2022.html
38 Thailand, (2019). National Security Policy and Plan. Web site: https://www.nsc.go.th/wp-content/uploads/2020/05/The-National-Security-Policy-and-Plan2019-%E2%80%93-2022.pdf
39 Trinidad, T., (2012). National Cybersecurity Strategy. Web site: https://www.enisa.europa.eu/topics/national-cyber-security-strategies/ncss-map/TrinidadandTobagoNationalCyberSecurityStategyEnglish.pdf
40 Uganda, (2014). National Information Security Policy. Web site: https://www.itu.int/en/ITU-D/Cybersecurity/Documents/National_Strategies_Repository/Uganda_2014_National%20Information%20Security%20Policy%20v1.0_0.pdf
41 United Arab Emirates, (2017). National Security Strategy. Web site: https://agsiw.org/wp-content/uploads/2017/04/UAE-Security_ONLINE.pdf
42 United Kingdom, (2016). National Cybersecurity Strategy. Web site: https://assets.publishing.service.gov.uk/government/uploads/system/uploads/attachment_data/file/567242/national_cyber_security_strategy_2016.pdf
43 Vietnam, (2016). Vietnamese Cybersecurity Strategy. Web site: https://cloudscorecard.bsa.org/2018/pdf/country_reports/2018_Country_Report_Vietnam.pdf

Glossary

Anonymization – relying on cryptographic anonymity tools to secure or mask an identity on the Internet.

Authentication – an effective method of verifying an identity, or other attributes of an individual.

Autonomous System – a compilation of IP networks managed through the routing system that is governed under the control of a specific entity or domain.

C.I.A. Triad – a system of confidentiality, integrity, and availability of services offered via the Internet.

Cipher – an encrypted message conveyed with programming language.

Commodity malware – software easily available for purchase, or free download, that is not customized and is used by a wide scope of various threat actors.

Cryptography – scientific analysis or study of encoding and deciphering codes and ciphers.

Cyberattack – callous exploitation of information communication technologies and digitally dependent enterprises and networks to invoke harm and gain control through known vulnerabilities.

Cybercrime – crimes primarily committed over the Internet that targets governments, businesses, financial institutions, academic institutions, and/or individuals.

Cyber domains – the perimeters of land, air, sea, and space where cyber activity is prevalent and deployed.

Cyber ecosystem – a correlated interconnected infrastructure, encompassing individuals, processes, data, information communication technologies, as well as engulfing environment and societal conditions that impact those interactions.

Cyber espionage – secretly gaining access to secure systems operated and managed by a government, Parliament, or Ministries to acquire information for nefarious purposes and monetary gain.

Cyber incident – an event that creates a penetrable presence or potentially poses a threat to a computer, internet-connected device, or network with the use of malware, Trojans, viruses, phishing, or unauthorized intrusion that disrupts normal computer and information systems activities.

Cyber resilience – effectively securing computer and information systems to have the ability to defeat cyber events and, if harm is caused, recover within a limited timeline.

Cyber security – strategic method of deterring criminal access and activity and usage of sensitive data and information within the physical, personnel, and operational boundaries within government, business, organizations, enterprises, academia, and individual computer and information systems, including cloud environments, artificial intelligence, quantum computing, Internet of Things, 3D printing devices, and robotics.

Cyberspace – the virtual domain of all cyber activities, including the Internet and satellite electronic data information transmission.

Cyber threat – a serious of virtual events or virtual action of attack that is unauthorized and unexpected and has the potential to cause or impose harm or an economic crippling.

Data breach – unauthorized access to computer and information systems that exposes sensitive information and intellectual property without authorization.

Distributed Denial of Service Attack (DDOSA) – malicious targeting of Web sites and increasing traffic volume to block traffic from accessing the Web site URL.

Domain Name System (DNS) – a naming system for computers, information systems, and network services defined in a hierarchy of domains.

E-commerce – electronic business commerce that involves trade, purchasing, and selling of services, products, and/or information in a virtual Internet environment.

Encryption – a concealment of plain text information enveloped in cipher text to prevent access and deciphering of data at rest and in transmission.

Incident management – the implementation of effective strategies to assess, record, and mitigate potential threats imposed within an enterprise, business, government, or academic environment that can compromise or cause harm to a computer or information system or network.

Incident response – procedures enacted to address both short and long-term unauthorized activities that impose threat or harm to computer or information systems, cloud environments, quantum computing, artificial intelligence, 3D printing, and the Internet of Things.

Integrity – assurance that data shared across the Internet is accurate and without distortion.

Internet of Things – the correlation of computer and information systems embedded within appliances, electronics, software, and sensors that communicate and transmit data across the Internet.

Malware – malicious software, or computer programming language coded to cause disruption to a computer or information system that is identifiable as viruses, worms, Trojans, and/or spyware.

Network (computer) – a host of computers compiled together with the sub-network or inter-network that enables the exchange of data across the internet.

Penetration testing – procedures deployed to test the security of a computer and/or information system to determine its ability to deter and/or stop successful unauthorized access to the secured data hosted on the computer and/or information system.

Phishing – utilizing email that looks authentic but deceives recipients into opening the malicious files often delivered as an attachment, disguised as weapons of destruction, embodying malware, viruses, Trojans, or spyware that is downloaded and installed onto a computer or information system without authorization.

Right to Be Forgotten – legal ethic that enables citizens to be removed from list that convey their personal identity and information from Internet searches and other directories. Active in Argentina, the European Union, and the Philippines.

Revenge porn – sharing explicit images, pictures, or video without consent i.e., written or verbal of the person in the images, pictures, or video to sabotage their reputation.

Ransomware – utilizing malicious software to block access to a computer or information system until a sum of monetary payment is rendered.

Service License Agreement – legal binding document conveying the responsibilities held by the manufacturer or service developer to the product purchaser that can be used in liable legal litigation. This agreement engulfs the service and/or product quality, availability, and responsibilities with a guarantee.

Script-kiddies – amateur computer programmers who use pre-designed HTML/HTML5 or other computer programming language software developed by others to hack computers and information systems with little to no experience.

Skimming device – the use of a small computer handheld device or equipment that enables downloading of credit card information from the bar code, chip, or self-service payment kiosk at gas pumps or ATM machines that store the collected data until the data can be transferred to a new fake credit card or information storage device.

Social Engineering – gathering information from people, systems, and resources to create an identity and/or to establish a compiled file of data on a subject.

Spear Phishing – sending fraudulent emails to someone using a name they can identify with hopes of acquiring access to sensitive information that can be used for fraudulent purposes.

SPECOPS – software utilized to block weak passwords and secure passwords with authentication management solutions.

Spoofing – modifying a known IP address, email address, or a phone call from its original source to trick the receiver into thinking it is from someone they know, to obtain sensitive data.

SQL – a computer programming language utilized for database management systems and for streaming in correlation with database management systems.

Trolling – instigating untrue ideology that seeks to acquire responses from people to invoke emotions of hostility or arguments commonly utilized in online social media forums and communities.

Virtual mobbing – sending electronic messages to intimidate someone and cause them pain or to invoke fear.

Index